Accidentally, a Book

Writings and Drawings

Accidentally, a Book
Andy Fuller

First published November 2023
Reading Sideways Press
Leiden, The Netherlands

readingsidewayspress.com
readingsidewayspress@gmail.com

This book is copyright. The copyright of the original text belongs to Andy Fuller. Except for private study, research, criticism or reviews, as permitted under the Copyright Act, no part of this book may be reproduced, stored in a retrieval system or transmitted in any form or by any means without prior written permission. Enquiries should be made to the publisher.

Typeset in Avara and Caudex
Designed by Amarawati Ayuningtyas

ISBN: 978-0-6454725-3-0

READING SIDEWAYS PRESS RSP

For Nuning and Cahaya

Table of Contents

vii Beforeword

1 And now, all that is gone: on the KITLV Reading Room

11 Athletes and Revolutions and Reviews

27 Earthly Agency, or, *The Nutmeg's Curse*

37 Gesekan Kata

51 I am busy until Wednesday

59 *Interlude*: Poverty Plague, by Afrizal Malna

71 On Learning Dutch

81 Repository of Memories

91 So-Called Asian Library

101 Towards: a letter to my mother on reading *Mullumbimby* by Melissa Lucashenko

111 Tourism

121 Urban Sensorium: the body in the city and the writings of Afrizal Malna

133 Utopia for Beginners

145 Afterword

151 Book List

Before-word

Every time I have a birthday I make a promise to myself: "This year. This year: *this year* will be the year that I publish a book. I'll knuckle down and get my dissertation published. I'll collect my articles on football in Indonesia and have them published." I then become another year older and the aforementioned ambition hasn't been realised. The dream always gets scrambled about one month in to my new age. Kurt Vonnegut might say, *so it goes*. I like this phrase for it seems to encourage one to be at ease with what is happening or has happened.

So, here is this book: *Accidentally, a Book*.

Unlike my unrealised plan to publish my dissertation on Seno Gumira Ajidarma (now ten years overdue – sorry, Seno), I started writing without a grand plan. Or, perhaps, it was only after having drawn a draft of the cover for this book, that I realised I was making a book. I did the cover first and then the writings were put into this frame of a book. I have now realised that, for me, a book is a framing of ideas. It is a frame within which one assembles different narratives which are somehow connected. *Accidentally, a Book* consists of my notes and essays or articles. Some have been published elsewhere; others not. I've added notes to some of the essays that were previously published.

This book is also an outcome of my interactions with my daughter, Cahaya. She often invites me to draw with her. Cahaya sits down at the table and can draw scenes quickly from her imagination. At a loss of what to draw and feeling often conflicted about what covers to use for Reading Sideways Press (RSP) books, I started to copy the covers of books that I had read or was reading or would like to read. Copying an image was easier than coming up with both composition and idea. One thing led to another and I ended up doing quite a few: many of which are in this book. Drawing the covers of books provided moments for thinking with the books and their voices and for re-materialising their aesthetics. I wondered if doing so would help me make decisions about what covers we could use at RSP.

In July 2023, RSP held a small event at KUNCI Study Forum and Collective in which we discussed our publishing practice. There were about a dozen participants: some old friends, some new friends, some current collaborators. We ended the session with each participant choosing a book from KUNCI's library and drawing its cover. We copied the images together; participants wandered around the room commenting on each other's drawing skills and asking about why they had chosen their particular book. Somehow the practice of drawing together lightened the mood, or functioned as some kind of conversation enabler; it took our conversations in unpredictable directions. We each had our portraits taken with our drawings at the end of the session; each of us was smiling, while holding our drawings. We didn't even put these photos up on Instagram: maybe it was too fun for that.

PLAYING CHANGES | Jazz for the New Century — Nate Chinen

And now, all that is gone: on the KITLV Reading Room

Or, the closure of the KITLV Reading Room[1]

The Royal Netherlands Institute of Southeast Asian and Caribbean Studies (KITLV) has suffered a major funding cut. The Institute, with its collection of some one million books and hundreds of thousands of other documents, images, maps and miscellanea, many of them concerning Indonesia, dates back to 1851, an era that also saw the founding of Leiden's Volkenkunde Museum (1837) and the Tropenmuseum (1864) in Amsterdam. This was the era of high colonialism, when many artefacts from the colonies could be easily transported back to the centre of colonial authority.

The KITLV collection is also home to many documents from Suriname, another colony of the Dutch.

---

1. This essay was first published here, *a long time ago*: www.insideindonesia.org/archive/articles/kitlv-reading-room-gone-collection-remains

To avoid possible dissolution, the KITLV recently made some compromises to reduce the cost of its services, such as the maintenance of its famous Reading Room. Over its last few months of operations, the Reading Room was decorated with notices in Dutch, English and Indonesian in bold type stating that its last day of operation would be June 27th.

Professor William Frederick from Ohio University, a long time user of the KITLV's collection, wrote a letter bemoaning its closure. The letter reflects the sense of attachment felt by the room's long time users: 'I have returned as often as possible over the years, and taken the more or less inevitable changes in stride: the retirement of coffee trolleys and service, the move to the Reuvenplaats, the banishment of the dear cat who often kept my lap warm on winter days in the Reading Room.'

The nostalgia in the letter dissolves into something more forceful: 'though some of [the initial proposals] were modified, I saw and continue to see, the remaining changes as a shameless and both intellectually and fiscally irresponsible savaging of a unique and priceless tradition, and of a peerless, world-class research facility.'

I carried out research in the Reading Room during its last months, and have fond memories of its routines. As I approach the building in the morning grey, a man stands by the doorway wearing brown leather shoes, a faded pair of jeans and a thick grey jumper. He's reading a print-out of a journal article. A moment later, a couple of staff from a neighbouring institute come in with a trolley and to remove a couple number of boxes of books and journals. Staff walk into the building barely looking up, a sense of purpose in their stride.

A moment later, after checking the clock, Rini Hogewoning unlocks the door to the Reading Room and says, 'welkom' to the waiting visitors, in a voice that is both proud and friendly. Rini has worked at the Reading Room for some 30 years. Her colleague, Josephine, commenced more recently. They greet visitors with a direct 'Morgen!' (Good morning) and perform their duties with an informal 'alsjeblieft!' (if you please!) and a smile. The Reading Room offers both the professional formality of a 'peerless' research institute and the informality that develops amongst well-known, familiar colleagues. It is a specialised environment designed to enable access to the KITLV's collection. It provides a space in which scholars can easily interact, and experience the occasional fortuitous meeting.

Lights hang low over broad desks: these are used for the reading of manuscripts and old texts, all of which happens within the gaze of the librarians. A line of desks face out on to the Witte Singel – one of the main canals that define the city limits of Leiden. There are machines for the consultation of microfilm at which scholars scroll forever downwards or horizontally. The Malaysian Studies room is somewhat more private and the door is sometimes closed. This room looks out onto a neighbouring basketball court and the activities of school children can provide some light entertainment for scholars in between writing or reading some text. The leisure boats gently float by on the Singel, another example of Leiden's quiet pleasures.

On one side of the room there are numerous computers for searching the catalogue. There are racks of newspapers from Indonesia and Suriname, behind which are the shelves of Asian studies and anthropological journals. Here one also finds popular magazines in Sundanese and Javanese which might be hard to find even in

Indonesia. Yet, here they are clearly visible and easily accessible. Newspapers from the previous week or month endure, proving to be less ephemeral than the events they describe.

'The KITLV moved here in 1975. There have been people who have been working here for a long time and each of them—each of us—are dealing with the situation in different ways,' says Dr Reinder Storm. As head of collections at the KITLV, Reinder is disappointed at the prospect of the Reading Room's closure. But he is also pragmatic. 'Much will be lost, no doubt about it. Some staff are looking for new jobs. But it is not as bad as it could be. The ambience will be lost and so will the ability of researchers to engage with the librarians who are so knowledgeable of the collection.' The KITLV is not the only grand institute in The Netherlands facing significant downsizing. The Tropenmuseum, Volkenkunde and Africa Museums are all now being managed by one central group of managers.

'When the collection moves to be handled by the University Library, the degree to which the documents are indexed will change. It is this information that makes the documents in the KITLV collection so easily searchable for users.

The management at the University, however, regard such thorough indexing as to be a waste of time and money.' But Reinder also acknowledges that it is more than this. 'When people use the reading room, they have a sense of community. Scholars in one place. That will be lost when visiting scholars will use the library or some other space at the university or KITLV.'

Reinder emphasises the importance of the work of the Reading Room's two most prominent and loyal staff, Rini Hogewoning and Josephine Schrama: 'But, most importantly, what is lost is that researchers won't be able to access the information and knowledge that is provided by Rini and Josephine. They can not only help people find particular texts, but, they are also vital in introducing researchers to other researchers who have similar interests. When the collection will be available through the University Library, researchers will pick up the books from the lockers on the ground floor. There will be no human interaction. And, if there is, it won't be with a librarian who has some 30-40 years of experience with a very particular collection.'

Reinder stresses that the collection will remain. This is in contrast with some of the rumours and stories that have been spreading about the KITLV, which have often taken on a doomsday-like narrative. 'It is not as bad as it could be' is hardly an optimistic and positive statement. Yet it is Reinder's persistent message. Some of the staff are being retained to continue to work at the University Library, others will be looking for work, while others will take the opportunity of an early retirement.

Alfred Schipper has been working at the KITLV Reading Room for 30 years. 'I have never been to Indonesia. But, maybe someday, I will.' Each morning Alfred could be seen walking from his office near the stairwell, to the elevator, unlocking it with a key, and then taking the very short, but slightly slow descent, to the floor below. His job is to bring the materials ordered by researchers through the library's catalogue to the Reading Room. His day is filled with many journeys down to the store where the books, CDs, DVDs, newspapers, maps, magazines and other paraphernalia are kept.

'Each day there are about 100 books that I take and return. Some days, there are more, some days there are less.' Alfred works to his own rhythm and system. The noise of the printer in his office, churning out the slips which name the books to be collected for library-users, contrasts with his quiet manner. The temperature below is maintained at around 17-18 degrees and the humidity is at 55 per cent. The silence of the store is broken only by the rolling of the trolley's wheels and the sound of the machine that tracks the changes in the temperature and humidity. The KITLV collection will remain in this store, but the books will now be transported to the Leiden University Library across the other side of the canal.

The KITLV has been downsized and there is some resentment and disappointment. Professor Frederick's letter is only one of a number of signs of this. He expresses something intangible: with the closure of the Reading Room, the sense of privilege one could enjoy in having such direct and familiar access to the KITLV's unrivalled collection is gone. Ten thousand visitors come to KITLV's Reading Room per year and now their interaction with the Institute has been shifted to the Leiden University library. The muted response of staff and users belies a sense of deep regret at the changes being applied to KITLV.

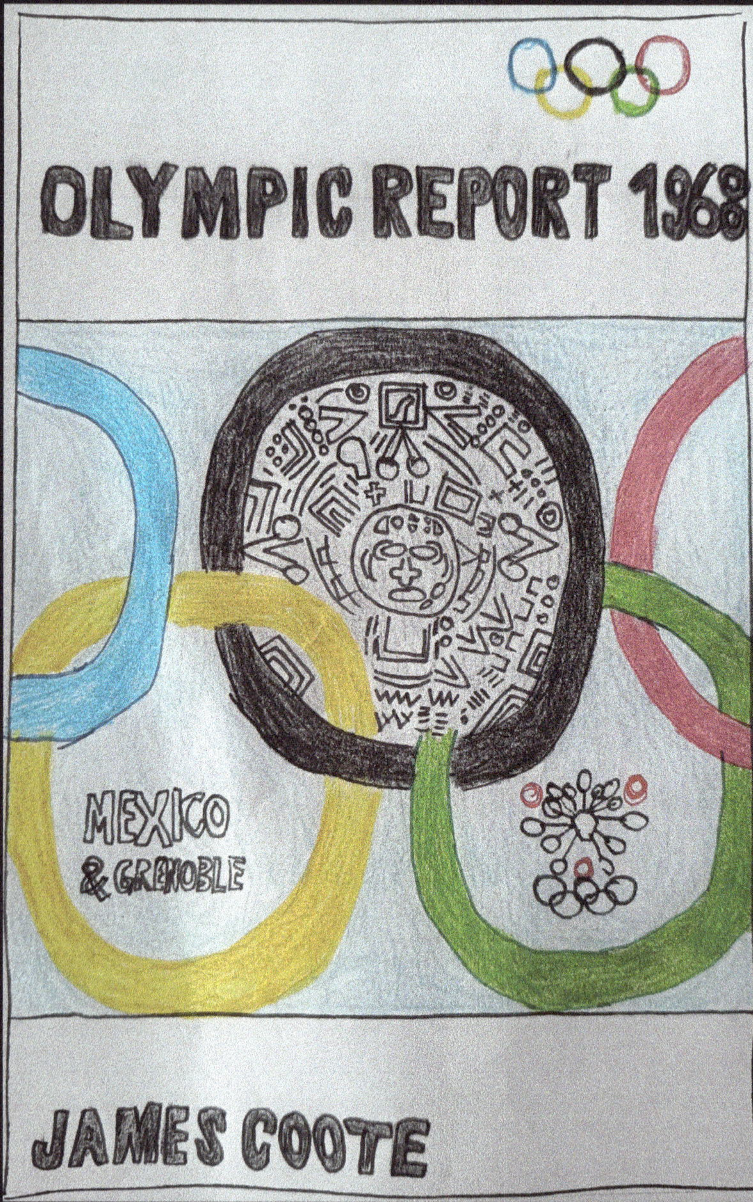
OLYMPIC REPORT 1968
MEXICO
& GRENOBLE
JAMES COOTE

Athletes and Revolutions and Reviews

I have occasionally written book reviews for academic journals. It's a way to get a 'free' book and to turn one's reading into some kind of output. But, I have promised to write more reviews than I have actually ended up writing. This is yet another kind of writerly guilt. Or, at least another anxiety: *the anxiety of the article one hasn't written*. But, now, at least as someone who publishes other peoples' books, I'm getting my own back: others promise to review, we send it to them, but they don't end up doing so. *No problem.*

And then, a review is published; or even a prize is awarded, but this doesn't necessarily matter one jot. It doesn't make the author famous and the books don't fly off the shelves as a result of the review. Nonetheless, for some authors it perhaps gives them a sense that their work has been recognised.

Just prior to the start of the Pandemic, I contacted the editor of a sports studies journal to say that I'd be willing to review, *The Revolt of the Black Athlete* by Prof. Harry Edwards. Before the Pandemic had fully managed to disrupt the mail system, the book arrived at my doorstep. I read the introduction and put it on a shelf close to where I would sit and read updates on how many people had contracted Covid. The book remained firmly on the shelf; I had relegated it to the very much cluttered 'later' pile in my mind. I then got a postdoc in the Low Lands and my immediate interests swerved away from sports/politics.

After two years of knowing in the back of my mind that I hadn't actually reviewed the book that I said I would, the editor politely contacted me and said: 'oh, by the way, we are still waiting on your review.' I said something about, 'better late than never' and that it would soon be on its way. I read the book (it was shorter than expected) and wrote my review, but it still took me another further month to send it. Perhaps this was an expression of separation anxiety in textual form. I wasn't yet ready to let the editor have it. But then I was due to travel and I wanted it done prior to departure. I got it done: it went out through the outbox.

**

The Revolt of the Black Athlete: 50th Anniversary Edition, with a new introduction and afterward, by Harry Edwards, Urbana, University of Chicago Press, 2017, xxiv + 232 pp., USD$29.95 (hardback), ISBN: 978-0-252-04107-5

The reissuing of this book, with its new introduction and afterward, is part of the argument Edwards is making. The gap of 50 years since its first publication and 2017 is a framing device to make arguments about what happened in 'the past' and what is happening presently. The discourse that Edwards develops are particularly relevant to the English-speaking sporting contexts. Although the book is bound to cases from the US and the Black Power movement, the analysis remains vital for developments in sporting politics elsewhere – perhaps the UK and Australia in particular.

In the introduction Edwards makes several key points which bring a new contextualisation to both the original text and to contemporary discourses. Edwards, a distinguished and revered professor, also gives moving retellings of his formation as an academic/activist. For Edwards, this is living of the American Nightmare, a term he borrows from, the novelist, James Baldwin: "to be black and to be aware is to live the American Nightmare". He was black and living what for white Americans would be 'the American dream': a prestigious university scholarship and on the brink of a successful sporting career. Being at the intersection of sporting/ intellectual achievement gave him particular agency and insight into the sporting hypocrisies of the US and the ability to critique them.

In the words of Edwards's colleagues, he was regarded as being a 'successful Negro'; an epithet which was also repeated in sporting contexts. They would be 'tolerated' and 'celebrated', if they performed well and kept their mouths shout; but if such athletes spoke of the racism they encountered/experienced daily, their careers would be soon ended. In the US, this is repeated through the experience of Colin Kaepernick, in Australian football, there is the case of Adam Goodes: a much lauded player, until his so-called activism created too much discomfort amongst a sports watching public who only want to marvel at the movements of black bodies, but are less enthusiastic about listening to Black stories.

The breadth of time between the first publication and this re-issuing has enabled Edwards to make a few poignant and stringent observations. One of these is in regards to 'history': who gets listened to and what is remembered. Edwards's analysis of the proximity of college sports to 'the plantations' as present throughout the book, at the time gave fuel to his opponents to label him as a 'black militant'. That some of his detractors would (much) later make a similar claim and without acknowledging his position points to some of the immovable structures which shape who is listened to and what experience, insights (etc) is regarded as being knowledge.

The book is furnished with one of the most striking images which encapsulates the intersection of sport and activism. Tommie Smith and John Carlos] stand, heads bowed, with each one of their arms raised aloft, fits enclosed in gloves, making the black power salute. Cropped out of the picture though is Peter Norman, the silver medallist, who not only still holds the Australian 200m record, but earned Smith and Carlos's enduring respect for his solidarity with them. Smith, Carlos and Norman would all be ostracized from their national athletic fraternities. Smith and Carlos would later pay their respects to Norman as two of his pallbearers when he died in 2006.

Much of the force of this book rests with the author's instrumentality and proximity to the events that he analyses. Edwards was in the thick of the political activism. While many of the chapters read as detailed criticism of the unfolding dramas, without necessarily being buttressed by 'the relevant literature', this may also be because Edwards's work was indeed pioneering this field. If this book has not already become compulsory reading for researchers of sports and politics, this reissuing makes it even more so.

Edwards's retelling of the events leading up to and during the 1968 Olympic Games in Mexico is one of more the striking chapters. The conflict, unfolding drama read like a playbook of more recent politically charged sporting controversies. There is the direct confrontation of Edwards towards Avery Bundage and the galvanising of support between Black America and Black Africa. Edwards also emphasis the OCHR's support for the people of Mexico as they seek to resist the 'Uncle Tom' government which is enabling the Olympics. He gives the details on the context of Smith and Carlos's actions and how they followed through on their commitment to not celebrate their achievements. Other athletes, who sought to find a compromised position, out of their fear for the possible sanctions, wavered and adopted a celebratory demeanour. Edwards, for example, excoriates George Foreman for his comfort within white-America and for his waving of the US-flag (p.85). He writes, "his behaviour was in the interest of white-folks". As in the newly added afterward, this chapter is also enriched by the inclusion of letters addressed to Edwards in which his activism is acknowledged from various allied organisations.

The afterward provides Edwards's commentary on more recent developments. Edwards's experience of having lived through and been a pivotal player in sports-based activism pro-

vides him with probably unparalleled authority for such commentary. He outlines the trajectory of 'waves' of activism, from initial strivings to Black Activism which speaks to issues beyond matters of racism. The emergence of the Black Lives Matter movement just prior to the books' reissuing further adds to the weight of this book. While Edwards is supportive of the full-spectrum of black athletic 'activism' (or otherwise) he says this on the BLM movement: "The Black Lives Matter movement can fuel, frame, inform, and even inflame activism, but with no definitive measures and markers of legitimate progress, as was the case with Black Power, it leaves its adherents open to a wide range of outcomes, including co-optation, confusing symbolism with substantive change, and pursuing goals that do not produce significant change in institutional culture, or in the control and application of power" (p.161).

This book is essential reading for students of the history and intersections of sports and politics. It shows the entanglement of racist and colonial ideologies within the governing bodies of mega sporting events. The book no doubt can be recreated but with using FIFA as the target.

Edwards's style is passionate and thoroughly rhetorical. There aren't any moments when one is left unclear about where he stands on a particular matter. This deeply convinced style makes it readable to a general audience. The many documentary sources and appendices make it a valuable resource.

**

The Mayflower Bookshop has moved up and down Breestraat several times over the last few years. Now, they seem to have settled on a convenient location, next to the lane where H&M is also located. There is much window frontage and many passersby. *Foot traffic.* On sunny Saturdays, it is filled with tourists and students. I was in there once to gaze at the new paperbacks – perhaps to buy another *Diary of a Wimpy Kid* for my daughter – when I fortuitously saw a new line of hardcover books in the sports section. An Englishman, who had a career as a marathon runner in the late 1960s, had taken up a job in the Hague, where he had lived for most of his life. He had passed away and the Mayflower Bookstore had acquisitioned his collection. There were about ten first edition, hardcover

books on long-distance running training, published in the 60s and 70s. They were in pristine condition.

SZ, one of the owners of Mayflower, had set the prices which ranged from about 16euros to about 40euros. I politely asked the staff to set a bunch of them aside for me as I couldn't quite immediately work out which ones to buy. Titles included: *Run to the Top* by Arthur Lydiard and Garth Gilmore; *The Lonely Breed* by Ron Clarke and Norman Harris; *The Golden Mile* by Herb Elliot (as told to Alan Trengove); *Athletics: How to become a Champion*, by Percy Wells Cerutty and the *Olympic Report 1968* by James Coote. The books are artefacts of another time: these are anglo-centric, heteronormative and are written for a British empire audience. You have to be male, stoic and tough. The coaches are dour and humourless. I bought them nonetheless: I wanted to see how far training advice had come. I had also been told that much of the training I have followed can be traced back to Arthur Lydiard's methods of high weekly mileage and, where possible, hill training.

The main reason I bought Olympic Report 1968 was for its possible account of the Black

Power protest. Coote writes in his chapter: Student Riots and Black Power (pp.22-30):

> There was no I.O.C. member at the Press Conference after the rostrum incident when Carlos and Smith spoke of the attitude towards negroes in sport – "People recognise me as a fast nigger but that still means I'm a nigger," said Smith, while Carlos said, "We are great Americans for 19.8 seconds; then we are animals so far as our country is concerned," and both tried to give the reasons for their side of the story. Typically, the I.O.C. did not ask them why they had done this. They were only concerned that they had "brought politics into sport" – as if two young Americans could really have brought politics into sport any more than it is already there." (Coote, 1968, p.28).

When I had bought the book, I had spoken about the Black Power salute moment and of my interest in it. The bookseller at the time had never heard of the incident or seen the image.

Earthly Agency: or, *The Nutmeg's Curse*[1]

A red dust enveloped the city. The hot winds brought the dust into the suburbs. Temperatures rose into the high 30s and low 40s. The red dust blanketed the city's buildings and dampened the strength of the sun. The north wind continued to bristle through the suburban trees. Smoke from distant fires drifted into the city. In my street, somehow, a neighbour's house seemed to be on fire. We had stayed indoors to avoid the heat: but then I remember my mother rushing outside to see what was happening. I couldn't grasp it. The city, suburban Melbourne, was no longer a

---

[1] Most of this essay was first published here, https://www.queenslandreviewerscollective.com/2023/04/29/the-nutmegs-curse-by-amitav-ghosh/

> *refuge. I felt two conflicting emotions: this was some kind of horror and, at the same time, 'everything is going to be alright'. It was the first moment, in retrospect, when I could feel that the beautiful, romanticised, but maladjusted and malpracticed austrayan landscape could turn on those who didn't listen to or work with it.*

I am reading Amitav Ghosh's book, The Nutmeg's Curse. *Yes, I am.* It is a book for a reading group, which I am sometimes a part of, the Anthropology Book Club, at Utrecht University – founded and run by anthropologist Tessa Diphoorn.

**

It all starts from a noise: startled Dutchmen sense their vulnerability in the distant Eastern Indonesian island of Lonthor, one thing leads to another and they soon seek to wipe them out from their homeland. The Dutch were seeking to establish a monopoly on the trade of nutmeg: one of the spices that gives the name 'the Spice Islands' to the region of the Moluccas in Eastern Indonesia.

The man behind the efforts to wipe the people of Lonthor off the map was Jan Pierterszoon Coen. He was an ambitious and ruthless man who saw both a great opportunity to enrich himself and the Dutch East India Company (VOC). Ghosh regards him and the Company as being pioneers of capitalism which is inextricably bound with colonialism, the logic of genocide and the will to extract natural resources and to render the landscape passive. The VOC demands a trade monopoly with the Bandanese; but they reject this as it would disrupt their relations with their neighbours.

Ghosh, an anthropologist by training, draws heavily on rich and varied textual resources. He retells the stories of others with the perspective of an insider; his writing evokes the feeling of *being there*. The scope of his reading is enriched by his visit to the Banda Islands albeit some time prior to the book being published.

Ghosh uses the story of nutmeg as both a symbol and literal example of iterations and practices of colonialism. He relates his argument across centuries and disparate geographies. He draws on the narratives of First Nations peoples' to counter ideas about landscape, place and nature. Somewhat remarkably, Ghosh tells these rather entangled tales without falling into the use of obfuscating academic jargon. Indeed, it is his will to stay concrete and specific in his story-telling that makes the stories he tells, so vivid.

Ghosh uses his chapter on 'Vulnerabilities' to highlight discrepancies in the north-south, rich-poor nation divide. He points to wealth as hardly being a determining factor in predicting the ability to climate induced disasters: pointing to the relative wealth of Italy and some US cities. Moreover, some nations of the global south sent medical staff to global north nations to help them during the COVID-19 Pandemic. Climate change shakes up apparently stable relations and established ideas about where capabilities and knowledges lie.

The anecdotes and specifics of the book are compelling. While the Dutch reign in the Eastern Islands (and elsewhere) became more and more violent, nutmeg was represented in paintings as specimen only: nothing was to be depicted of the violence wrought against its people and landscape alike.

For all the urgency of Ghosh's argument, it is a narrative patiently and convincingly told.

He argues for the dire need to find an alternative to capitalism with its inherent colonising and depleting, extractive logic. This is a beautifully written collection of 'parables', thickened through deep research. It is unnerving through the problems it analyses while also inspiring through its proffering of alternatives to avoid putting ourselves at greater risks of impending climate disasters.

**

I was at my computer; it was a Saturday and I was doing some editorial work. It had been a week of plus 35 degrees temperatures and on that Saturday, the forecast was for an even higher temperature. While working, I had the weather website open and at every few minutes I would check back to see the temperature climbing. It was some kind of spectacle. Sitting beneath the fan, knocking back grapefruit juice with ice, I felt comfortable, feeling that I was safely separated from the potentially catastrophic events that would likely take place elsewhere. The scale of rampaging bushfires have become a norm of the brutalised austrayan *landscape. Only in the wake of these bushfires or floods have First Nations knowledge bearers been consulted on how to manage and live with the land, rather than to extract it to smithereens. 'The nutmeg's curse' is like a new term with which to describe the denying of the earth's agency and for the will to only regard as something which can be extracted .*

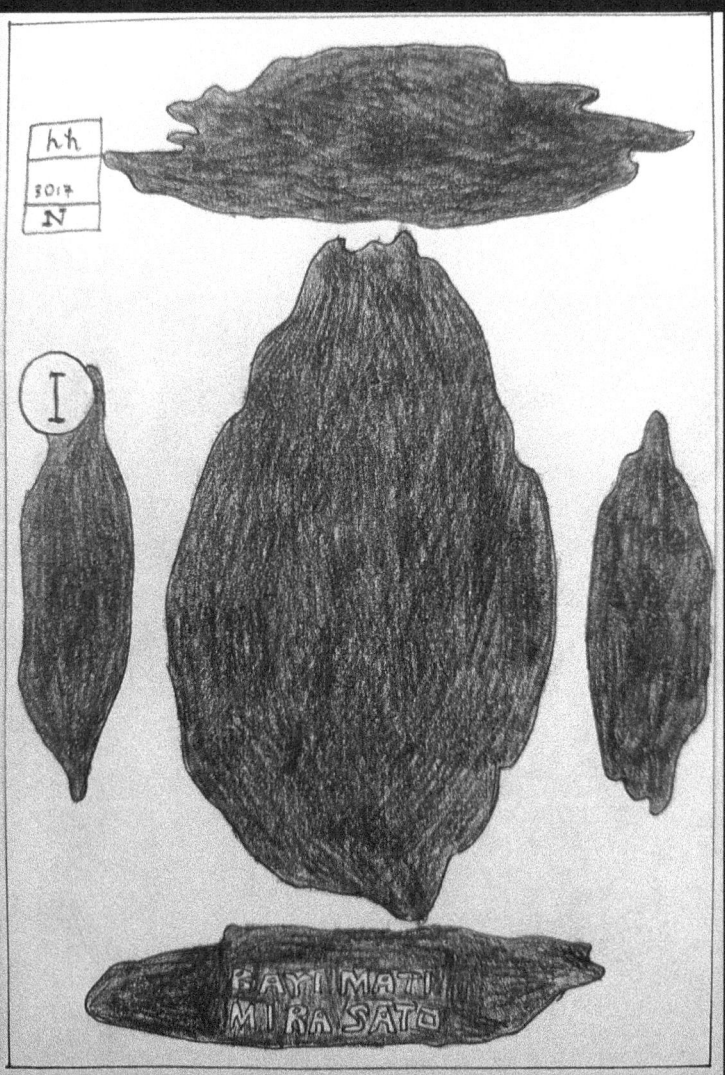

YANG BERDIAM DALAM MIKROPON

Kumpulan Sajak Afrizal Malna

Gesekan Kata

"Aku menangis karena orang dewasa
tidak mengerti apa-apa."

Ziggy Zezsyazeoviennazabrizkie, *Di Tanah Lada*

Saya selalu mengingat saat pertama kali saya membaca karya "Keroncong Pembunuhan" oleh Seno Gumira Ajidarma. Saya sedang berada di kamar tidur saya di sebuah rumah di Medan, pada tahun 2000. Cerpen itu, yang begitu, pendek, sederhana dan jelas memukau saya. Entah mengapa. Gaya bercerita Seno memberi gambaran yang tajam terhadap beberapa nuansa politik dan sosial. Beberapa tahun kemudian saya menulis disertasi saya tentang karyanya Seno. Lama kelamaan kami juga menjadi teman, walaupun tidak begitu sering berkomunikasi. Tulisan dan karya Seno menjadi semacam 'pemandu' bagi saya untuk membaca bagian dunia ini yang dinamai 'Indonesia'.

Saya juga ingat pertama kali saya membaca karya Ziggy Zezsyazeoviennazabrizkie: saya berada di dalam sebuah taksi di Jl.Cikini Raya dan pada waktu itu saya sedang menuju ke café Bakoel Koffie untuk menemuinya. Agak mepet, memang, tapi saya berusaha secepat-cepatnya membaca awal dari buku *Semua Ikan di Langit*. Saya sudah bayangkan dia akan bertanya apakah saya telah baca bukunya atau tidak. Saya mungkin, agak berbohong, yang mungkin begini, 'ya, saya sedang membacanya … sudah separuh'. Tapi, saat ketemu langsung dengan Ziggy, yang lagi asyik menulis di laptop saat saya tiba di kafe tersebut, saya tidak ditanyai hal tersebut. Obrolan kami berjalan lancar dan kami berbagi cerita kami masing-masing sebagai pembaca: siapa yang kami menikmati membaca. Dia sebut Neil Gaiman, saya sebut Kurt Vonnegut, dia ketawa. Dan selanjutnya. Dari beberapa kalimat pertama buku *Semua Ikan di Langit*, saya sudah langsung menyukainya. Dan, dalam soal sastra, saya selalu mengikuti hati-nurani saya. Saat membaca sebuah buku untuk pertama kali, saya tidak mau bersikap terlalu kritis. Suka, lanjut. Kalau nggak suka atau bosan; berhenti.

Di antara dua penulis ini ada seorang Afrizal Malna. Saya bertemu untuk pertama kali di lapangan parkir TIM. Sekarang, TIM berwujud baru; sudah direnovasi dan pegawai budaya sudah disediakan fasilitas yang lebih bermartabat. Di tempat parkir, kami berjabatan tangan dan Afrizal tersenyum. Sebuah senyum, yang mungkin hanya berlangsung sekilas, tapi penuh kehangatan. Mungkin saya jatuh cinta dengan dia pada saat itu. Nama 'Afrizal Malna', pada waktu itu, sudah cukup legendaris, sebagai tokoh dan sebagai penyair. Apa peduli dia dengan seorang asing, yang tiba-tiba nongol di depannya dan menyapanya. Lama kelamaan saya menerjemahkan karya dia sebagai *Anxiety Myths* (Lontar, 2012; terima kasih kepada orang tua saya, yang mendanai penerbitan buku ini) dan ikut menerjemahkan *Morning Slanting to the Right* (RSP, 2021; dengan sebagian dana dari LitRI yang sekarang sudah menjadi sebagian dari puing-puing pendanaan sastra). Lebih memuaskan lagi, sebagai salah satu pendiri penerbit RSP (bersama partner saya Nuraini Juliastuti), kami menerbitkan *Document Shredding Museum* (trans. Daniel Owen, 2019) dan buku Afrizal dalam Bahasa Indonesia,

Lh-2247-NI

Iwan Simatupang

MERAHNYA MERAH

SEBUAH NOVEL

GUNUNG AGUNG - JAKARTA MCMLXXVII

Prometheus Pinball (2021). *Promotheus Pinball* dapat pengakuan dari majalah *Tempo* sebagai salah satu buku terbaik pada tahun itu.

Saya tidak pernah memiliki cita-cita menjadi seorang penerjemah andalan. Pasti banyak sekali yang lebih berbakat. Bagi saya, tugas penerjemahan adalah sebagian dari proses menikmati membaca karya fiksi atau non-fiksi dan meniliti sesuatu. Dalam proses penelitian, saya sering menerjemahkan tulisan fiksi dan non-fiksi, sekalipun itu ditulis oleh 'penulis sastra' atau orang yang tidak menyebut diri sendiri sebagai 'penulis'. Tentu saja, cerita yang menarik, atau dengan kata lain, 'menarik perhatian kami ke arah lain', seringkali tidak berasal dari penulis sastra. Karya sastra tidak memiliki semacam monopoli atas narasi atau cerita yang patut dibaca, diberi perhatian ataupun, kalau ada penerjemah, diterjemahkan. Baik fiksi maupun non-fiksi yang ditulis dalam begitu banyak jenis wacana membantu kami memahami bagian kecil dari dunia ini; mengingat sesuatu, mendambakan sesuatu, dan sering mengajak kita untuk bersikap kritis pada pelbagai macam atau jenis kekuasaan.

Dari tiga penulis yang saya sebut di atas, karya mereka masing-masing memandu saya ke ranah yang berbeda-beda. Seno menjadi pemandu saya untuk memahami sikap kritis terhadap politik Order Baru. Dari karya dia saya bisa melacak atau mengeksplorasi hal semacam pembunuhan misterius, kekerasan negara terhadap rakyatnya sendiri (di Aceh, Timor Timur dll), apalagi Seno sendiri bersikap kritis terhadap rezim Orde Baru, tapi juga euforia reformasi yang memang tidak menuai semua impiannya. Tapi karya Seno bagiku, tidak berakhir pada cara saya memandang 'sesuatu Indonesia' (kata Afrizal); tapi karynya membantu saya membaca 'negara saya' yang diberi nama 'Australia': sebuah negara colonial settler; yang didirikan atas perampasan hak Orang Asli atas Tanah mereka.

Karya Afrizal beranjak dari titik awal yang berlainan dengan karya Seno. Buku-buku Afrizal mengajak kita untuk merasakan dengan segala 'kemampuan sensibilitas' kita; untuk merasakan apa itu 'urban'; untuk mengerti bagaimana kota telah menjadi sebagian dari tubuh kami dan sebaliknya juga. Bagaimana, Bahasa Indonesia memisahkan kita masing-masing dari bahasa dan ingatan. Dan sekaligus Bahasa Indonesia ini berperan juga dalam penciptaan dan pemaknaan pengalaman kita dengan dunia urban yang kita jelajahi sehari-hari. Karya Afrizal begitu sensitif, atau memberi perhatian khusus pada barang, tekstur, bau, tubuh dan perkotaan. Karya dia sering terasa terisolasi dari kenyataan tapi juga lahir dan hidup di dalam ke-terisolasi-ian itu.

Karya Ziggy membuka dunia sastra baru bagi saya sendiri. Sebagai pembaca, saya tidak pernah terbawa ke dunia yang diciptakan oleh Ziggy. Mungkin pembaca lain sudah membaca karya 'seperti' karya Ziggy sebelumnya. Tapi, bagi saya, tidak ada 'seperti karya Ziggy': bagi saya, karya dia adalah sesuatu yang sepunuhnya baru; sepenuhnya asli (walaupun saya tahu hal ini nggak mungkin). Saat saya membacanya, saya merasa terbawa ke dunia baru. Bukunya benar-benar berperan sebagai alat untuk berkelana dalam imajinasi. Saya pernah bicarakan karya Ziggy dengan beberapa 'peneliti popular culture Indonesia' yang bekerja di Australia. Mungkin saya tidak usah sebut nama mereka karena mereka berbicara dengan santai dan *off the record*. Tapi momen ini memang sangat memberi kami semacam insight pada cara pandangan seseorang. Dua-duanya mengambil sikap yang merendahkan. Ahli #1: "karya dia tidak begitu istimewa. Biasa-biasa saja. *Hohum*." Ahli #2: "Does the book have anything specifically about Indonesia in it?" So-called Ahli (orangnya sudah jadi professor) Nomor 1 membuat saya sebal karena dia bisa melihat betapa saya bersemangat untuk karya Ziggy. Apa maksudnya untuk merendahkan karya Ziggy, kalau orang lain ini sedang nge-fans pada karya Ziggy? Ahli #2, yang menduduki posisi mapan di Universitas Melbourne, ternyata hanya tertarik pada karya 'sastra Indonesia' yang membawa 'ke-Indonesia-an' secara 'eksplisit' ke dalam teksnya. Sepertinya seorang penulis yang lahir dan dibesarkan di Indonesia (di Lampung dan Jakarta) masih kurang 'Indonesian' bagi peneliti, yang kebetulan seorang yang bukan orang Indonesia [*laughing emoji*]. Kedua orang ini tampak begitu *tidak* penasaran, *tidak* begitu terbuka pada penulis baru.

Dan sentimen kedua orang ini mengingat saya pada sebuah kutipan yang sangat offensive dari John McGlynn (sama saja dengan Lontar): "publishers aren't looking for you, they're looking for Indonesia." Saya sebagai peneliti wacana dan budaya urban; sebagai orang yang pernah menerjemahkan karya yang ditulis dalam Bahasa Indonesia dan sebagai orang yang pernah buka penerbit kecil (dalam arti, belum mampu menjadi besar), tidak merasa begitu. Peran saya memang tidak penting. Saya hanya seorang asing yang sebetulnya kurang lama tinggal di Indonesia. Tapi saya melihatnya begini: yang penting bagi saya bukan ke-indoensia-an seseorang. Karena memang peneliti, penerbit dan penerjemah tidak berhak untuk menentukan atau membingkai atau memberi definisi yang jelas dari arti kata itu. Saya memang mencari suara yang berbeda dan tersendiri – sekaligus 'suara baru' juga muncul dari sebuah konteks dan ekosistem yang luas. Saya hanya pernah membaca sedikit sekali dari apa yang disebut 'sastra Indonesia'. Dan saya semakin sadar bagaimana saya semakin tidak peduli dengan istilah itu. Penulis yang lahir entah di mana di Indonesia memang tidak bisa dibatasi oleh berbagai macam alat pengklasifikasikasian yang membuat karya mereka lebih gampang terjual di pasar.

Weaving of Worlds: a Day on île d'Yeu

Greg Lockhart

I am Busy Until Wednesday

'I am busy until Wednesday. I can't meet you until then. I have stuff on.'

He is wearing thick, round glasses and is somewhat slumped in his chair behind the computer at the bookshop.

There is a glass wall behind him and a narrow alley leading which connects the Nieuwe Rijn to Breestraat. Here passers-by stop to browse the large format photo books and best sellers in the windows.

Jorge Carrión writes, "the Best Bookshops in the World Aren't the One You think They Are." I like this title, Olaf says when I pass it to him to scan.[1]

---

[1] In Jorge Carrión, *Against Amazon and Other Essays*, trans. Peter Bush, Windsor: Biblioasis, 2019.

This bookshop is barely the best bookshop on Breestraat. It is one of at least four. Each time I come back though I find myself a new book.

I only buy one book per day.

**

'The Tina Turner book sold well. The Sinead O'Conner memoirs not so much.'

**

The bookshop has moved up and down Breestraat for much of its life as the owners look for the most strategic positioning.

**

'You haven't sent me a message.' 'Yes, but I'm here now and I'm asking you when you are able to meet to talk.' 'Send me a message. It's your book.'

**

The staff at the shop grow steadily and Olaf is sorta new. I tell him I'm writing a short book and want to briefly talk with him.

I come in to the shop in the mid-afternoon: I ask, how many books have you sold today? About 53 via the real shop and 20 or so online. We talk and some customers queue behind me. They're almost silent and I keep on talking.

**

'I guess Huyzinga was one of the last great Dutch public intellectuals. I think he lived in Oegstgeest. He is buried there.'

**

The desk is large and it supports a mix of best sellers, small-sized books, some classic, second hand Penguin paperbacks and some picture books. There is also a glass cupboard in which are stored hardcover, first editions: some may be signed. There is a price tag of 75euros for one book: hardly prohibitive for a collector, but also a step up from the bookshop's 3 for 20euros deal which covers much of their paperback stock.

**

'I sent them an email saying that I was into books and sooner or later I heard back from them and then I started to work here.'

'I don't know what I will do afterwards. Maybe there will be no afterwards and I'll just keep working here. Maybe I will work for a publisher. That would be nice.'

**

He stands out the front of the shop and smokes cigarettes, occasionally.

**

'I read the classics. But I'm not reading many novels at the moment. I tend to get too affected by them. I'm kind of a bit emotional that way.' 'I saw Wende at Lowlands and I somehow cried. Not sure why, but the Dutch bands and musicians who sing in Dutch are so much more interesting than those who sing in English. We were camping. Tickets were some 300 euros. It was both exhausting and exhilarating. There was a 24 hour stage.'

**

He is sitting behind the counter, wearing a moustache and a shirt. He writes for the Leiden University newspaper.

**

Everyman

PHILIP ROTH

City Life from Jakarta to Dakar

Movements at the Crossroads

AbdouMaliq Simone

R
Global Realities

Interlude:
Poverty Plague[1]
By Afrizal Malna

The imagining of poverty can be described through the wages of historical and strategic sectors: that is, the daily wage of Farm Workers (Buruh Tani) and Construction Workers (Buruh Bangunan). The daily wage for Farm Workers in December 2020 was IDR 52,510 (about 5 USD); and that of Construction Workers was IDR 85,807 (about 8 USD).[2] The wages of these sectors reflect the gap between Farm Workers and Construction Workers as a representation of the gap between the village and the city. The wage forms a latent trap where poverty becomes a plague.

The life in this novel has a distance of some 20 years from the description of wages above.

---

1 Translated by Andy Fuller, February 2023

2 BPS, 2021

The novel is set in the context of Jakarta's urban poor who interact with the Urban Poor Consortium (UPC) in the period after the 1998 Reformasi movement.[3] Poverty is represented through a sectory of society which has been isolated as a result of the public policies of the city government. How are have they become entangled in spider's web of poverty?[4]

In 1997, Indonesia was hit by an unusually long dry season. The nation's economy was heading into recession. The political situation was also intensifying: Suharto was heading into his fourth decade as president. More and more people were finding it hard to make ends meet. Prices for staples were skyrocketing. The various

---

[3] When I was a child, I lived in Senen, Central Jakarta, in a poor area. My memories of this time are recorded in a collection of my poems, *Prometheus Pinball* (RSP: 2020). I returned to the world of the urban poor as an activist between 1997 and 2003.

[4] The term 'deprivation trap' was coined by Robert Chambers and it refers to poverty itself, physical weakness, isolation, vulnerability and a lack of agency. See, for example, Robert Chambers, Pembangunan Desa, Mulai Dari Belakang (Jakarta: LP3ES, 1987). Ragnar Wilhelm Nurkse called this the 'vicious circle of poverty': there is a backwardness, imperfect marketplace and a lack of funds which lead to a low productivity rate. This results in the inability to earn a decent wage, which results in low rates of saving and investing, which leads to being marginalized, and so on. In Yulianto Kadji, "Kemiskinan dan Konsep Teoritisnya", https://repository.ung.ac.id/hasilriset/show/1/318/kemiskinan-dan-konsep-teoritisnya.html

crises affected all layers of society and many people lost their jobs.

In rural regions, opportunities for employment were diminishing. Young people from villages started to look for opportunities in cities where they could access education and employment, albeit with limited funds. In cities, they lived in illegal settlements: next to rivers, besides trainlines, beneath overpasses and cemeteries. The only kinds of work they cold access was in the informal sector: as *becak* drivers, itinerant food sellers, buskers, sex workers, rubbish collectors and scavengers.

The informal sector is subjected to multiple aggressions from the city government. The workers' habitats are destroyed, razed or burnt down. But they never disappear. Informal workers disappear for a moment and then re-emerge in accordance with changing social conditions.

In Roanne van Voorst's book, *The Best Place in the World* (2016), which was published 11 years after this novel, there is a clear evocation of this plague of poverty. The book is based upon Roanne's fieldwork from living in a poor area of Jakarta. Their life was so precarious and the occupants were so vulnerable that Roanne opted to use pseudonyms as a means of protecting the identities of people in her story as well as the name of the area in which she worked. When Roanne had returned to the Netherlands, she received news that the kampung in which she had worked had been razed. Isolated spaces of poverty are prone to being razed in a violent manner; rather than being ameliorated in a humane way. The kampung that is present throughout this novel was also razed prior to the novel's publication.

After the *reformasi* movement of 1998, the urban poor gained a moment to fight for the informal sector as a part of everyday life and culture, alongside the formal sector. Their rallying cry was "a city without eviction".[5] They were fighting for the rights of the urban poor to gain equal access to housing, education, health services, the economy and politics. In reality the city has grown through both the formal and informal sectors. The informal sector continues to develop its alternative culture as a means to escape the plague of poverty.

---

5 The term "penggusuran" encapsulates both "eviction" of people from their homes as well as the razing of their homes. I use both terms depending on the context of the sentence.

In the shack of a *becak* driver in a dense kampung by the river banks of the Tanggul Jagung river in Teluk Gong, North Jakarta, the foul stench of the dirty river comes in through the windows and through the wooden floor. The shack is on stilts and juts out onto the river. The shacks in this kampung are as small as 3 x 3meters; each used by one family. It's like a hotel with a narrow corridor which separates the small rooms on either side. Durng the day, the rooms becomes places in which to work and cook. In the evening, they are a shared place for sleeping.

The alternative accommodation is a kind of "emergency management" as a means to endure one day to the next in the face of potential eviction, flooding, fires, while also working in whatever capacity to fulfil their daily needs. Behind this emergency management can be found many ideas, strategies and memories in facing crises as a kind of collective knowledge which can't be found elsewhere. Then they are evicted and their houses are razed, this kind of collective knowledge also disappears.

In the city government's vision of the city, there isn't an idea about the intersection of the informal and formal sector. There is no formulation of how the city can be managed together, which creates a kind of absurdity.[6] This absurdity forms the surrealist context in which the novel is written. That the plague of poverty doesn't come from the poverty itself. But rather from the form of power which uses power as the language of truth in implementing its governance.

On the 30th January, 2023, some seventeen years after this novel (Lubang dari Separuh Langit), the Minister for State Resources and Bureaucratic Reform, Abdullah Azwar Anas, mentioned a budget of Rp.500 trillion for overcoming poverty. This extraordinary budget, which is of a total different scale to that of the minimum wage for labourers, evaporated during ministerial meetings and accommodation costs used for comparative studies.[7] Such practices indicate how poverty is not just an economic problem, but also a kind of plague which is rooted in how power is understood as the language of truth.

---

6 The original uses 'batas absurd'.

7 See: Adi Suhendi, "Anggaran Kemiskinan Rp 500 Triliun Sebagian Besar Habis untuk Rapat, DPR Akan Panggil Menpan-RB", Monday, 30th January 2023 07:10 WIB, https://www.tribunnews.com/nasional/2023/01/30/anggaran-kemiskina…liun-sebagian-besar-habis-untuk-rapat-dpr-akan-panggil-menpan-rb

Power is implemented and blindly ignores the limits of power itself.

I didn't previously imagine that I would write this novel. Mainly because the plague of poverty has given birth to its own way of thinking and its own language. These are different from the languages which have shaped me. Different smells, colours, spaces and movements. Everything moves in a straight line between creativity and the crisis of survival. The steps are short, rather than long-term. The steps feel complicated and weaken one's resolve.

After Tanggul Jagung was razed, for some reason, I started to write this novel using my handwriting. I wrote it so quickly. It only took me one month of writing day and night. I wrote it while staying in Apuan, Bali, in the village of the painter, Made Wianta.

This English language version of the novel has taken another step. I don't know why Hannah and Jorgen like this novel. I feel that this novel isn't nice to read and begs the question: 'what is my right to write their lives?'

I thank Hannah Ekin and Jorgen Doyle for translating this novel. I also thank Andy Fuller and Reading Sideways Press for publishing it. I thank Made Wianta and his family. I particularly thank the people of the Urban Poor Consortium and in particular those of Tanggul Jagung, whose homes have been razed. My deepest respect is for them.

Afrizal Malna

Sidoarjo, 12 February 2023

Winner of the Nobel Prize in Literature

HERTA MÜLLER

THE HUNGER ANGEL

'A terse, hypnotic, moving novel'
New Yorker

BRIEVEN AAN DE PRINSES

On Learning Dutch

I am learning Dutch: well, *sort of*. I go to lessons once a week. In the room with me are other semi-locals: folks who are here for the short term, mid-term, not-sure-how-long-term. We are united by our sense of 'may as well try to learn some Dutch' – even though it is unclear of its practicality. People say: 'you don't need to learn Dutch. The Dutch speak such good English!' At the drop of a hat, indeed, people *do* switch to English at the Hema or the AH whenever an unconvincing Dutch accent is heard. The practicality is in the emotional connection that speaking the language creates. Not so much as to whether it has some kind of direct, tangible outcome; *methinks*.

My neighbour says to me, 'lekker weer, he?' To which I reply, 'eindelijk'. And the next time we cross paths, I say to him, 'lekker weer, he?' To which he replies, 'eindelijk'.

I have a running friend, Bereket. He has lived in Leiden since coming to the Netherlands as a refugee from Eritrea. He once told me his story of his travels across land and the boat journey. He could have been a top level athlete. He also had a stint as a footballer. He's now an electrician: working long hours and coming to training already tired. We go for long runs together we ask familiar questions: alles goed met je familie? Wanner is je volgende wedstrijd? Heb je gisteren lekker gelopen? He wants to practice his English with me; like I want to practice my Dutch with him. He always understands my Dutch and never has a problem with my imperfect Dutch accent.

Today, I sent Bereket a message and said, 'ik heb een jas voor je'. *I have a jacket for you.* Sometimes my efforts at making Dutch sentences remind me of the proximity of Dutch to English. Het is niet voor mij. It is not for me. Etc etc. Which also reminds me of one of the best insults someone has given me about my efforts at speaking said language: 'Sorry, I don't speak English' was the reply after I had haplessly asked some question in 'Dutch'. So bad was my accent that my interlocutor didn't recognise the language.

**

The BPlusC library, in central Leiden, was getting rid of its rarely-used books. They were being sold at 50 euro cents a pop. I took the chance to pick up some popular novels that I had long-seen on bookshop shelves but had never actually bought or read: John Banville, *The Sea* and Philip Roth's *The Humbling*. I read them soon after, almost surprised about how much I enjoyed them. Relieved too that I no longer had the reader's anxiety of 'never having read anything by such-and-such author'. The library was also selling, seemingly much of its collection of simplified texts for Dutch language learners. Titles included: *Moord volgens plan* (Murder according to plan); *Duif, ik heb je* (Dove, I got you); *Werkloos* (Unemployed) and *Een nieuwe liefde voor dokter Hans* (A new love for Dr Hans). Brieven aan de Prinses (Letters to the Princess) though offered a different kind of text. The book is a compilation of short letters written by language students to Princess Laurentien who had facilitated the courses that they participated in. The letters are seemingly less about learning Dutch in particular, but more about gaining access to realms and spaces the writers felt otherwise cut off from.

Toen ik in Nederland kwam, kende ik geen Nederlands. Maar toen heb ik les gevolgd. Mijn leven is veranderd. Beetje bij beetje leered ik communiceren met mensen, op straat, op de markt, in de winkel, en kan ik een afaspraak maken met de dokter.

Taal is belangrijk. Door de taal onstonden problemen op school. Toen moisten mijn kinderen naar een andere school. Zonder taal kun je niks.

Als ik de taal niet een beetje ken, kan ik mijn kinderen niet volgen op school, ze niet opvoeden, en ze niet helpen als ze problemen hebben op school.

En de administratie thuis, veel papieren moest ik lezen, en dingen regelen voor betalingen, anders krijg je problemen of een boete. Doe je dat niet zelf, dan ben je afhankelijk van mensen en soms hebben mensen niet veel tijd voor joe. Kinderen helpen op school is ook belangrijk. Als je de taal niet kent, gaat het fout. De Nederlands taal is moielijk. Ik spreek hem niet perfect, en schrijven vind ik ook moielijk.[1]

---

[1] Eenvoudig Communiceren (ed.) (2010), *Brieven aan de prinses*, Amsterdam: Eenvoudig Communiceren, p.47

When I came to the Netherlands, I didn't know any Dutch. But then I started a course. My life changed. Little by little I learned to communicate with others: on the street, in the market, in the shops and I could make an appointment with the doctor.

Language is important. Problems arose at school through language. When my children had to go to another school. You can't do anything without language.

If i didn't know any language, my children couldn't follow the lessons at school; they couldn't get educated and we couldn't help them if they have problems at school.

I have to do a lot of paperwork for the domestic administration. I've got to organise a lot of things and pay for things; otherwise you will have problems or have to pay a fine. If you don't do that yourself, it means you are dependent on others, who don't always have much time for you. Helping the children at school is also important. If you don't know the language, things go poorly.

Dutch is a difficult language. I don't speak it perfectly. I also find writing difficult.

**

There was a student in the Dutch class and I couldn't quite place his language ability. Of all of us hapless half-locals, he was the one who could walk into the room, greet the teacher amicably, reply casually about his day and basically engage in quick, back-and-forth banter *at the right tempo* of a fluent speaker. Yet something shifted when he would be asked to read: he would stutter and utter words which weren't on the page. I couldn't make sense of this. Where he had been confident and fluent, speaking off the cuff, he became anxious and hesitant in pronouncing words he had only moments earlier uttered easily when having a dialogue with the teacher. It then became apparent that he had some kind of reading issues. The teacher, seemingly mindlessly of the hurt and embarrassment she would cause, then asked, during the class, 'are you dyslexic?' to which he avoided answering.

Novel

AFRIZAL MALNA

LUBANG DARI SEPARUH LANGIT

AKYPRESS

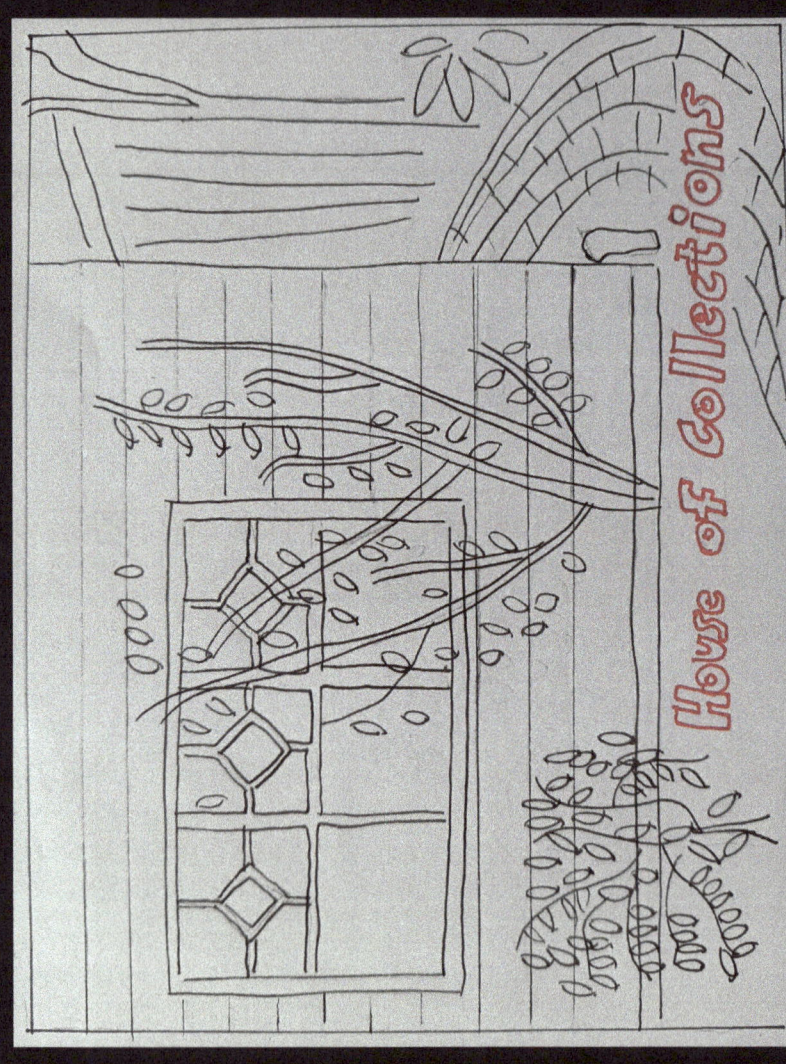

Repository of Memories

You can never go home.
          -cliché

There is a novel, *Life, a User's Manual*, which tells the stories of the inhabitants of an apartment in Paris, one character at a time. It tells the stories of the goods and belongings and materials; one thing after another. There is a hardcover, first edition copy of one of the biographies of aforementioned book's author, Georges Perec, standing in a glass fronted cabinet by the entrance to one of my parents' houses in Richmond in inner suburban Melbourne. I have read, *Life, a User's Manual*, but not yet the biography of Perec. I read it when doing my best to read great 19th and 20th century novels. The book faces outwards and I can see the portrait of the goateed Perec. He looks playful, for indeed he must have been. He also wrote a novel without the letter 'e'. The book is in the designated section of literary biographies of my father's collection. I also biographies on other 'great' writers: Borges, Burgess, Calvino, Lessing, Murdoch. Many others, too.

There is too, a photography book, *House of Collections*, by an artist and scholar, Claudia Terstappen. The book has no text. It consists only of photographs she took over a couple of days at Trev and Michele's old home in Glen iris – a quiet, unremarkable, middle class suburb of southeast suburban Melbourne. A leafy suburb with a train station and a tramline. Claudia was taken with how my parents had managed to line the walls with paintings. These walls were a veritable salon of Australian modernist artists. Many big austrayan names were there: James Gleeson, Robert Rooney, Rod McRae Dennis Passalick, Brett Colquhoun, Jonas Balsaitis, Robert Klippel (sculptures and collages). Sculptures filled the small empty spaces next to doors and couches. There was a Russian toy tower; there were small aluminium boats from a trip to Java.

VINTAGE CALVINO

IF ON A WINTER'S NIGHT A TRAVELLER

The house was a California bungalow and a friend of theirs had made a porch swing for it to make it complete. He couldn't stomach seeing a bungalow without a swing on it. The swing made the veranda in front of the house suddenly more useable, particularly for cool drinks on hot summer evenings. The swing would creak and the sound of it could be heard through the frame of the mosquito-wire door. Music from the CD player by the dinner table could also easily reach the veranda: Bob Marley and the Wailers, Kraftwerk, Brian Eno and John Cale, Laurie Anderson. There was a safe distance from the footpath the veranda was also separated by the front lawn and the high brush fence, a style my parents had brought with them from their home town of Adelaide.

You can never go home, indeed, but sometimes a book is made of the house in which you grew up and sometimes such a book aids memories and helps them come to the surface. Probably this is the function of Claudia's book for me. It is a book that was only printed on a small scale – perhaps it was simply a gift for Trev and Michele for she knew they were on the brink of selling it and moving on.

My father would write letters to politicians and authors with his fountain pen while sitting at his desk. He moved throughout the house: sometimes in the dining room – which was different from where we ate – to the study with the vertical, blue-lined wall paper, to his next study, which was my former bedroom, after I had moved out. The rooms of the house became more and more cluttered. Books went from being neatly ordered in shelves, to being placed in the gaps at the top of the shelves and on top of the shelves. The books then escaped the shelves: becoming stacked in piles; one on top of the other. All the while, my mother maintained an incredibly small footprint: one small desk with reading lamp and telephone, on top of which sat a couple of family portraits from a trip to Europe and another one from the austrayan countryside. My mother would place the novels she had finished reading on her dresser in her bedroom. She was modest in her collecting of books: one or two books at a time and each novel she bought, she would read. The bookshelves started to sag under the weight of the hardcover books my father insisted on collecting. He used naphthalene to keep away the insects. The naphthalene penetrated the chocolates we ate once at some kind of dinner event; Lindt chocolate mixed with mothballs never tasted so good.

The newspaper clippings couldn't be contained. They fell onto the floor in approximate piles: for it was a slow process of sorting and compiling and sticking into relevant scrap books. The unruly clippings also needed to be folded neatly into the scrapbooks to prevent unnecessary bulging or having unwanted scraps of paper poking out over the edges of the scrap book. I was often enlisted to sort and assemble these scrap books. There was something calming and focusing in this process. The scissors and the scraping as the metal cut the pages; the somewhat capricious behaviour of different brands of glue sticks. I started my own scrap books of images from one or two newspapers: I was looking for photographs which somehow represented interesting happenings in Melbourne's urban landscape. My father though filled rows of shelves with this clipping scrap books; these were like analogue google searches. And when his grandchildren were born, he now had a new audience to make the scrap books for.

It was the house in which the dog nearly died after getting blood poisoning. The house where I would so often win at table tennis and where

I would lose angrily. It is where the cat was buried on a winter's night. It is where I failed to learn mathematics and also where I wondered in drunk after parties a few times. It is where I had my first, awe-inspiring encounters with the female body. It is where I read Haruki Murakami novels and where I picked up Italo Calvino novels and appropriated them from Trev's collection into my own; hoping he wouldn't care. My mother would cook in the kitchen and tell me to turn off my music: Terry Riley's *In C* particularly triggered her. But we shared a love of John Cale's singing on the Velvet Underground's 1993 concert in Paris. The house was a 40 year project of my parents to assemble and cultivate their tastes; to collect works and to establish a network within Melbourne's art scene while simultaneously parenting their offspring.

A SUNDAY TIMES BESTSELLER

Jordan Ellenberg

HOW NOT TO BE WRONG

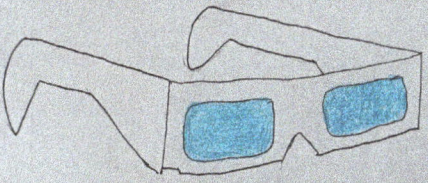

THE HIDDEN MATHS OF EVERYDAY LIFE

'A delight, full of simple yet deep insights about many areas of modern life.'
ALEX BELLOS, GUARDIAN

So-Called Asian Library

There is a reading room on the top floor of the University Library (Universiteit Bibliotheek, UB). Inside of this reading room, there are tall plants in deep tubs. Some of the plants almost reach up to the ceiling. This reading room is some fifteen meters back from the front of the building, but it is filled with light. Although the doors are closed and there are no open windows, the air is not stifling. The large windows at the front of the building, look out onto the Witte Singel and from here it is possible to look out over to the densely treed environs of the Hortus Botanicus which also encapsulates the *sterrenwacht* (observatory).

> *A mobile crane lifts a new piece of building onto the project site for the expansion of the library. There is scaffolding*

and temporary office spaces in which the staff and engineers sit and chitter chatter and pore over the plans in their high-vis vests. A man climbs up the scaffolding and shifts around chest-high, blue rubbish bins. The lights are flashing on the mobile-crane and cyclists and cars make detours around it on this curiously, windless – yet, typically overcast - morning.

The Witte Singel is narrow but there is seemingly enough space for two bicycle lanes and for vehicles to travel in both directions. It is a kind of thoroughfare that runs around the western side of the town centre of Leiden. It is lined with a narrow stretch of grass, trees and bushes along which humans take their dogs and where runners mobilise their legs. Inside this reading room, the air-conditioning hums at a constant din: there is also the sound of another person typing, for this room is strangely quiet. The semester hasn't begun. A staff member walks into the room and her footsteps squash gently into the thick, dense carpet.

From the red reading chairs on the ground floor in front of the borrowing shelves and service desk, one can look up and see, in somewhat out-of-place neon lighting the word 'Asian Library' – but the word 'library' is obscured. 'Asian'. This general term confuses something about the collection. It isolates and separates. It maintains an exotic, colonial gaze. And thus the book on the collection is titled, 'Voyage of Discovery' and Peter Frankopan, can speak euphemistically of '[Dutch] trading interests' as being the motivator for the study of Indonesian languages and cultures (p.12). Frankopan, *for what it's worth*, can barely hide his contempt for the humanities: "we can sometimes forget that great advances are not just made in the sciences, but in the humanities too" (p.13). Not bad gumption for an essay on a library; a collection. Maybe he thought his readers wouldn't somehow be otherwise favourably disposed to 'the humanities'. This volume, so proudly produced, is written from the collectors' perspective. There is a glaring absence of Indonesian voices and contributions from Indonesian scholars.

Writing some time ago, Ariel Heryanto made this argument in his article 'Can there be Southeast Asian in Southeast Asian studies?':

> it is no longer forgivable for outsiders to engage in any scholarly endeavor in this

area study without some consideration of the unequal relationships between them and those they study. There has been a general consensus on the need for expanding further the space and respect for Southeast Asians as speaking subjects and fellow analysts, rather than silent objects of analysis, although there is diversity in the degrees and kinds of such attitudes among Southeast Asianists outside Southeast Asia (2002).[1]

The plants in the glass-walled reading room have been borrowed from the Hortus Botanicus – one of the city's showpiece museums – for it functions so well also as a space for recreation and wandering. It is a semi-public space in which users go about their gentle activities of reading, strolling and observing the plants. Here in this reading room the plants are yet another degree of separation from where they originated. They are indeed living like museum pieces. But I am not going to pretend I don't enjoy being present here. It is *silenter* than elsewhere; my shoes

---

[1] Ariel Heryanto (2002), "Can there be Southeast Asians in Southeast Asian Studies?", in *Moussons*, No.5, 2002. See: https://journals.openedition.org/moussons/2658#ftn12

squeak on the marbled floor; the pages of the book scrape as I turn them and there is a minor, dull thud when I place my book on the low black chair which is next to the low, red chair on which I sit.

In her book, *In the Shadow of the Palms* (2022), Sophie Chao writes of the Marind's refusal (or rejection?) of the idea of taking animals on as pets or cultivating a garden. The plants in this reading room can't even feel the wind moving through their leaves, branches. Their roots are contained within the deep black tubs. It feels as if the isolation of these plants has been perfected. It is some kind of antithesis of the concept of forest or trees-as-networking beings. The spaces of the UB form the frames around which readings are made. Here, the plants, distended from one another, are pointers to their long travels from far-away places (an Indonesian elsewhere) and have become reference points for the imagination of users of the so-called Asian Collection.

Digital Minimalism

Choosing a Focused Life in a Noisy World

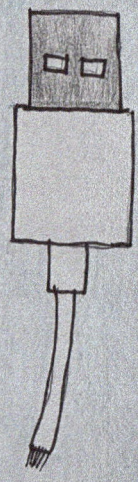

Cal Newport

'Brilliant, endlessly rich... pairs well with *1984* or *The Handmaid's Tale*' John Green

Parable of the Sower

OCTAVIA E. BUTLER

WINNER
QUEENSLAND
LITERARY AWARDS
BEST
FICTION
2013

mullumbimby

melissa lucashenko

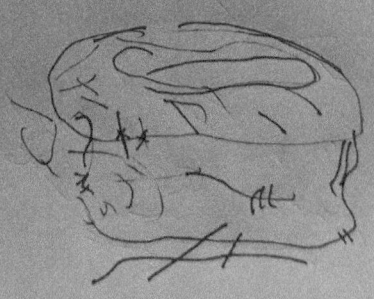

Towards: a letter to my mother on reading *Mullumbimby* by Melissa Lucashenko

18th November 2024
2e Kortelangestraat 4A
3121AB, Leiden
The Netherlands

Dear Mum,

I am reading Melissa Lucashenko's novel, Mullumbimby, *yes I am.* This sentence is adapted from Walter Benjamin's famous essay, Unpacking my Library (in his collection, *Illuminations*), which starts with the sentences: 'I'm unpacking my library. Yes, I am.' The essay tells of Benjamin's material encounters with his books. The bookishness of his books. Their weight and their origins; his will to categorise and order them.

> The books are not yet on the shelves, not yet touched by the mild boredom of order. I cannot march up and down their ranks to pass them in review before a friendly audience. You need not fear any of that. Instead, I must ask you to join me in the disorder of crates that have been wrenched open, the air saturated with the dust of wood, the floor covered with torn paper, to join me among the piles of volumes that are seeing daylight again after years of darkness, so that you may be ready to share with me a bit of the mood. (Benjamin, 2015, p.59)[1]

Benjamin's fascination with collecting reminds me of Dad's persistent and wide-ranging collecting. I also think of his diligence in maintaining his and your collection: previously using naphthalene and now more recently bathing them in eucalyptus oil, as you mentioned. When I think of Dad, one of his characteristic postures is trudging slowly up Richmond Terrace with a thin tote bag carrying the weight of perhaps a dozen second hand, hard-

---

[1] The essay is available here as a pdf: http://www.ruthieosterman.com/wp-content/uploads/2014/03/walterbenjaminunpacking.pdf

cover books bought in inner city Melbourne. The heaviness of these tomes was embodied in his slow walk: which would no doubt differed greatly from the speed of his walk to the bookshops, propelled by his enthusiasm about finding some kind of unexpected book to further enrich or broaden his collection.

But yes: I am reading *Mullumbimby* by Melissa Lucashenko. *Really, I am.* I bought this book more than three years ago: 12th February, 2020. *So long ago - even Covid had barely hit.* I had made two false-starts on it: the presence of two different bookmarks reminded me so. But this time I have made it more than half-way, so I feel, this time, I will see it through. Mullumbimby is an actual place on the (google) map. But there is this actual disclaimer at the start of the novel: "This novel is set mainly on the Arakwal lands of the Bundjalung Nation. Like the characters, however, the specific locations of Tin Wagon Road, Picabeen and Lake Majestic are entirely fictional. They exist only in the author's imagination." This last sentence though is a little disingenuous: through writing the novel, the places the author writes of become part of the 'reader's imagination', too. Through reading this novel, I now feel that, at times, I occupy those textual places. Probably partly because they resonate to a degree with some of my lived life: the scenery and the characters and the language is not too dissimilar to what I know through my experience of austraya.

The plane took off and owing to the temperature of the on-board air-conditioning, I had draped the blanket over my head and shoulders. It was the late afternoon outside and a gently orange sunset was happening. I didn't have the window seat and thus couldn't steal glimpses of the land below. But I had also made up my mind that I didn't want to take one last glimpse at the Continent. I wanted to make myself get used to the idea of austraya only being in my head through memories or (literary) imagination. I knuckled down and calmly read, one page at a time. I would save myself the luxurious of listening to music or a podcast or watching an airplane film for later in the flight. *Jo works at a cemetery. She is a former musician; she is divorced and has a moody teenage daughter on the brink of mental health issues. Jo owns land, which she has reclaimed and is on her traditional Bundjalung country. She falls in love with a handsome young dread-locked dude, whom she knows will give her trouble,* in the end. *Her beloved horse,* Comet, *drowns in a flood after getting caught in barbed wire which had drifted onto her property. Thus, big conflict with the neighbour and her own investigations into how ownership and land has been divvied up after colonial settlement. She leaves Mullumbimby to get a quick break from the drama of her horses death and the conflict with her neighbour. Her boyfriend comes along for the ride, but she is not thrilled with his company.* And that's about where I'm up to.

What I'm finding compelling, in part, about this novel is the way in which Jo, the protagonist, grapples with the presence of fences in the landscape. After the death of her horse: "she rediscovered, too, that every small part of the ridge, and each acre of the low-lying land along Stoney Creek, each field and paddock and roadside had not simply been named and claimed by the whitefellas. The taking of the land had been more absolute and thorough than she'd realised. Jo found that the pieces of land, dismembered each from the other, the orphaned parts of a now-dissolved whole, were to be found on the maps all *numbered* in the way that the graves at the Mullum cemetery were numbered in her groundkeeper's register" (Lucashenko, 2013, pp.133-134).

I'm applying this perspective to the stone fences we saw on the way to Dunkeld in Gariwerd; presumably built by so-called settlers. I imagine how foreign these fences/walls would have been at the time of their building. Nothing is so useful as a fence to make a claim for private property or ownership of land. Humans are beings who are beholden to the land: and its misuse, degradation and misappropriation ends in nothing but tears. Floods, droughts, bushfires turn this truism into some kind of vast, horrific spectacle.

Anyway: it is evening now and I'm a long way from Gariwerd. I can imagine you reading on the leather sofa in Richmond; perhaps falling asleep and then waking up and watching a bit of TV before asserting 'there's nothing on'. I wonder what novel you are otherwise reading.

MARCO KUSUMAWIJAYA

2005
A
3/86

JAKARTA

Metropolis Tunggang-langgang

In the Shadow of the Palms

Sophie Chao

More-Than-Human Becomings in West Papua

Tourism

Two pianos sit back-to-back in the front room of a bookshop which mainly stocks English language books. The score is open, showing a couple of Dutch-language songs. Perhaps the owner practices in between quiet times at the shop. Running a second-hand bookstore is part business acumen, part enthusiasm and part act of curatorship. The pianos, the owner says, are half of the business. They range in price from 400euros to 900euros. This is Leiden and much of its image and self-regard is based on its learnedness and sophistication. It is famous for its law, medical and so-called Oriental studies. *I walk along narrow streets and see the collections of owners, neatly arranged and climbing towards the ceiling.*

Here, a second-hand bookstore appeals to enthusiasts on the cheap, collectors and connoisseurs. *Time spent slowly at the shelves.* In the front rooms of apartments and houses of this city, one sees small pianos as a regular part of the kitchen or living spaces. The libraries of Leiden University and various research institutes hold a deep attraction for scholars. Weekly semi-leisure activities are shaped around attending guest lectures, doctoral defences and inaugural professorial lectures.

Tourists visit Leiden to stroll through the alms-houses, boat slowly along canals, or to eat ice cream along the Nieuwe Rijn on the off chance that it is not raining. When it is raining or cold or windy - which it is often enough - there are many cafes which emphasise cozyness (gezellig in Dutch) as their main strength. The coffees are weak and the hot chocolates are warm and mild - but do come with plenty of whipped cream, if requested. A tourist brochure recommends Leiden as a place where one really needs to spend more than one day to get to know.

Residents, of course, have ample time to get to know the minutiae of everyday Leiden.

A bookshop provides one such place for review. Stocks change slowly, as does one's taste. Opportunities for bargains slip through one's fingers and rare finds are made only occasionally. Purchases are made based on rarity, edition, cover, texture, taste and the values invested in the work at hand. Books become artefacts beyond their literary and textual qualities.

The customer, perhaps those who regards themselves as little more elevated, might search only for hardcovers, first editions and first printings. Others may value the simple designs of Penguin Classics or the loud designs of 1970s or 1980s editions of works by Anthony Burgess or Kurt Vonnegut. A book should not be judged by its cover, of course, but, a cover can be judged for its aesthetic qualities. And this the owner of Mayflower bookstore knows: for he has devoted a table to the books he likes with the covers that he likes. The books sit face up: the currency of the author's name and the book's title complemented and empowered by the aesthetics and design of the cover.

Paperbacks, in such cases, don't lose out to hardcover editions – most of which have their dust jackets missing. These are books that fit comfortably in one's pockets: they take on a soft and comfortable texture. At this store, they cost about the price of two coffees. On this occasion, I bought three books. The three books are, to varying degrees, popular classics: Jaroslav Hasek's *The Good Soldier Schweik* (trans. Paul Selver), Raymond Chandler's *Farewell My Lovely* and Kurt Vonnegut's *Timequake*.

The shop has a three for the price of two, so, they cost me about fifteen euros more or less the same as a cheap pair of winter gloves from Hema supermarket or two copies of the Times Literary Supplement. The books, outside of their narratives, contain information regarding their contexts in which they were published.

Hasek's novel, the oldest of the three, speaks most clearly of its trajectory as a read and re-sold book. The last page of Schweik provides an over view of the forthcoming series to be published under the imprint of Pelican. The first sentence is: 'We have long planned a companion series to Penguin Books and, with the end of paper rationing, we can now launch the Pelican Books.' Paper, in this case, is a kind of luxury. Now, with the advent of tablet readers, paper is a burden: something to get rid of; something that unnecessarily weighs down one's bag.

NEIL GAIMAN

American Gods

The book takes on the qualities of having been well-read and well-travelled. The spine is bowl-shaped, the paper is brown and easily torn. Yet, there are no dog-eared pages. There are also traces of its trajectory into this shop: The name of a previous owner, written in a blue ballpoint, has been erased and the sticker of a bookshop in nearby Oegstgeest remains on the inside cover. The book's original price 25 US cents is printed on the back cover.

One of the comic drawings by Joseph Lada is on the front cover. This contrasts with the current austere style adopted by Penguin Classics in their most recent printings. This book is no doubt easily downloaded. Yet these physical, tangible pleasures would be lost through such clicking and Googling.

This English-language bookshop in bookish Leiden has its own and newly established niche. Indeed, the current owner took over only in the last year or so. The owner knows that by appealing to the aesthetic qualities of popular paperbacks he is able to tap into an audience that enjoys the smells, touch and histories of a copy of a many-printed book. Paper is heavy and becomes easily damaged and marked.

It's fragile and expensive. Borrowed and downloadable books or articles and newspapers are all well and good for daily reading fodder. Some books, those that are particularly delightful 'for their cover, touch or memories' however, become a part of making a home.

A Life

ITALO SVEVO

VOLUME 3 IN THE
UNIFORM EDITION OF
SVEVO'S WORKS

Prometheus Pinball

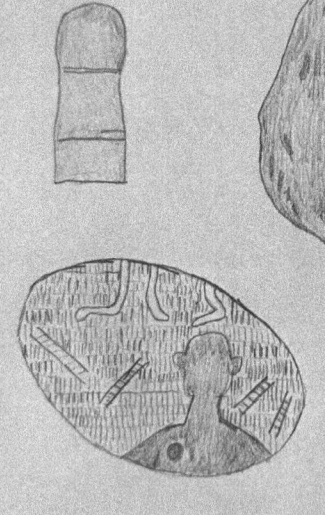

Afrizal Malna

Urban Sensorium: the body in the city and the writings of Afrizal Malna[1]

Afrizal Malna sits apart from many of Indonesia's contemporary poets. Not only is he a productive literary and theatre critic,[2] Afrizal has also written novels and collections of short stories. Afrizal, now in his mid-50s, is highly industrious: he writes around the clock, he travels regularly throughout Indonesia for seminars, readings and festivals, and when not working on a new collection of poems, he is revising older works, or having essays published in *Kompas*, a daily national newspaper. In 2012, Afrizal had

---

1 This essay was first published in The Newsletter, No.65, Autumn 2013 (IIAS, Leiden). Translations are by the author. RSP has since published Daniel Owen's translation of this book as *Document Shredding Museum*.

2 See, for example, his books Sesuatu Indonesia: Esei-Esei dari Pembaca yang Tak Bersih (Yogyakarta: Bentang Budaya, 2000) and Perjalanan Teater Kedua: Antologi Tubuh dan Kata, Yogyakarta: iCAN, 2010

residencies in Poland, at Platform Lublin, and at DAAD in Berlin. His most recently published book of poems is *museum penghancur dokumen*.[3] In 2014, he will return to Berlin for a year-long residency. During the 1980s and 1990s he was active with Teater Sae. For a period in the 1990s, he was affiliated with the activist group 'Urban Poor Consortium in Jakarta'. Despite this degree of activism, as a writer and poet, Afrizal remains relatively neutral in terms of Indonesia's often polarised literary communities.

Afrizal 's voic e as a poet is distinctive from others who are also well-established in the modern Indonesian literary canon. He stands in contrast to the wildness and joie-de-vivre of Chairil Anwar (Afrizal though, also writes of his indebtedness to Anwar), the intellectualism of Goenawan Mohamad (to whom a poem is dedicated in his new collection – pointedly or not), the activism of the legendary late W.S. Rendra, the gentle romanticism of Sapardi Djoko Damono, the playful domestic scenes of Joko Pinurbo or the absurdity of Sutardji Calzoum Bachri. Afrizal, if such generalisations are relevant, is

---

[3] All page numbers for excerpts in this article refer to: Afrizal Malna. 2013. museum penghancur dokumen, Yogyakarta: Garudhawaca.

concerned not so much with the romanticism of a poet's loneliness, but with a questioning of language and a bodily engagement with public and private space, objects and their associations. It is through the appearance of everyday objects that Afrizal's poems emerge as a vital catalogue and repository of the cultural meanings of space and things in Indonesia's everyday contestable modernity. In an essay which appears in *museum penghancur dokumen*, Afrizal writes:

> in the triangle between language, body and space, the poems in this collection are like a net that leaves behind what can't be caught in the net; i.e. shadows from the aforementioned triangle: linguistic-shadows, bodily-shadows, spatial-shadows. (p.106)

Afrizal's poems employ various strategies that evoke both a familiarity and a defamiliarisation with the objects of everyday life. His phrasing and grammar is often disarmingly simple. Yet, grammatical variation and poetic effect is achieved through idiosyncratic uses of words such as tentang (about), or di antara (in between). Moreover, he will often times remove subjects from sentences. This presents problems for translation, but, also opens up a broadness of interpretation and meaning.

Afrizal's poems draw on the practices of surrealism and montage. Objects are placed in the same sentences as each other without any apparent correlation. In these cases di antara, or just antara [space between/among], is used. For example, in Capung di atas pagar tinggi [dragon fly on a high fence] he writes, "seperti ada bangkai yang terus dipuja dalam warna kelabu langit, kenangan di antara kacang hijau dan bunga matahari" [like there is a corpse that is continued to be praised in the grey sky, memories amongst mungbeans and sunflowers] (p.12). And, in Musik Lantai 16 [Level 16 Music], he writes, "senda-gurau antara koper dan puisi, antara gigi dan daging tersayat, sebuah orgasme yang membuat seluruh bahasa manusia terdiam" [laughter between suitcases and poetry, between teeth and sliced meat, an orgasm that silences all of mankind's languages]. 'In between' or 'amongst' is used as a device to create relationships between disparate objects, and between concrete and intangible nouns. Surrealism, as Ben Highmore argues, is something more than just a formal technique epitomised by the "chance encounter on a dissecting table of a sewing-machine and an umbrella". But it is able to "attend to the everyday" through refusing to inhabit a separate realm between art and everyday life.[4]

Afrizal's sentences vary from being self-contained to those that are fragmentary and incomplete. And thus, he plays one sentence off against another. Afrizal writes in blocks of sentences, rather than flowing, linear narratives. They are repetitive and disconnected. This is a style of writing that embodies doubt in the language that he uses. Afrizal argues that he is 'uncomfortable' with language. And that despite being a poet, critic, novelist, he feels more at home with the discourses and practices of the visual arts.[5] He claims that Indonesian is his only language, but, that it is a language without a home; a language that rejects domestication. At his book launch for *museum penghancur dokumen* [6] he argued that Indonesian is his first language (and only language), but that it is not his mother tongue.

Afrizal's frequent references to the soles of feet and to the palms, emphasise the im-

---

[4] Ben Highmore referencing Comte de Lautréamont, in Highmore, B. 2002. *Everyday Life and Cultural Theory: An Introduction*, Routledge, p.46

[5] Discussion with Afrizal Malna, Café Lidah Ibu, 4 July 2013, Yogyakarta

[6] Cafe Lidah Ibu, Yogyakarta, 4 July 2013

portance of touch in his engagement with the space he occupies. He seeks to reclaim a kind of Indonesian language that is both questioning of its construction and grammar, as well as a language that draws on the body and physical experience, as opposed to bureaucratisation and staid formality.

Afrizal's poems often involve a fragmentary and multiple 'self': saya or aku. This first person presents the poetic discourse across various moments in time. Saya or aku is neither stable or reliable, but an entity that is diverse and problematic. Using these terms is a moment of contestation and negotiation. *Mesin penghancur dokumen*, for example:

"Ayo, minumlah. Tidak. Saya sedang es kelapa muda. [...]Saya tidak sedang nasi rames." [Go ahead, drink it. No. I'm being a young coconut juice. [...] I'm not being nasi rames.] (p.31) And, elsewhere, in Aku Setelah Aku [Myself after Myself],[7] the aku that is present is persistently problematic, never just 'aku', but always 'aku setelah aku' – as this self, or rather these selves,

---

7 Afrizal Malna. 2013. 'Aku Setelah Aku', in Aku Setelah Aku, unpublished collection, p.11. This is a collection based on his travels and residencies in Europe during 2012 (Poland, Germany and France)

negotiate an encounter with a woman in an unnamed city, somewhere in Europe.

The concluding essay from *museum penghancur dokumen* articulates Afrizal's position regarding the first person. He writes,

> the first person has passed at the moment a person writes. Writing is performed through changing the first person into the third person. I cannot write 'I' into time and space at the same time: the camera cannot photograph the camera, my eyes cannot see and gaze at myself at the same time. Writing only happens when 'I' has become 'him'."(p.102)

Nonetheless, aku and saya consistently appear throughout his poems. But, these are selves that are doubted and negotiated with the context of time (un-linear) and space in which 'aku' is a part.

The sense of an ambivalent imagining with Indonesian language is complemented by Afrizal's problematic relationship with Jakarta. The trajectory of modern Indonesian literature is inextricably linked to the processes of urbanisation and Afrizal's poems offer another variation on the ongoing exchange between urbanisation and the articulation of these changes through literary discourses. Afrizal's sense of disconnect with Indonesian is reflected in his realisation of the 'city' as a place that is not a site of 'return' in Indonesian literary discourse. He argues that to return never means to go home to a city. Although this statement is somewhat exaggerated and generalised, his point is that the city is most often imagined as a site of expectation, novelty and ambition. Afrizal, however, characterises his experience of Jakarta through the riots of the Malari incident (1974) and reformasi (May 1998). On the night of the Malari incident, Afrizal was woken by a member of the army as his home was searched for looters. It was at that moment that poetry became no longer a literary matter to him, but one of a "bodily engagement with space".[8]

Afrizal Malna's work as a poet spans some thirty years. His first collections of poetry *Abad yang Berlari* (1984), *Yang Berdiam Dalam Mikropon* (1990) and *Arsitektur Hujan* (1995) were written at the height of the Suharto-led New Order era. Until now, he has maintained

---

8 Afrizal Malna. 'Kota di Bawah Bayangan Api', *Kompas*, 17 March 2013, p.20

a consistent style – which some regard as being uniquely 'afrizalian'. In my reading, this afrizalian style draws on the techniques of inscribing a fragmentary self, an engagement with language games in which various punctuation marks are absent and subjects or objects are removed or rendered ambiguous. His diction frequently draws on the ideas of what is 'stored', 'kept', 'held', 'preserved', 'retained' through the use of the word menyimpan. The poems are explorations of bodily engagements with his surroundings: those of domestic and urban spaces. References to the telapak kaki [sole of the foot] and telapak tangan [palm of the hand] recur frequently. Afrizal's practice of constructing poems from lists, from playing with uses of 'in between' and 'about' are other common traits. Afrizal's poems, however, cannot be reduced to these qualities and techniques. Through drawing on these practices, Afrizal's poems maintain a fine balance between consistency and variation, which asserts his distinctive poetic voice.

Kraftwerk:
Future Music
from Germany
Uwe Schütte

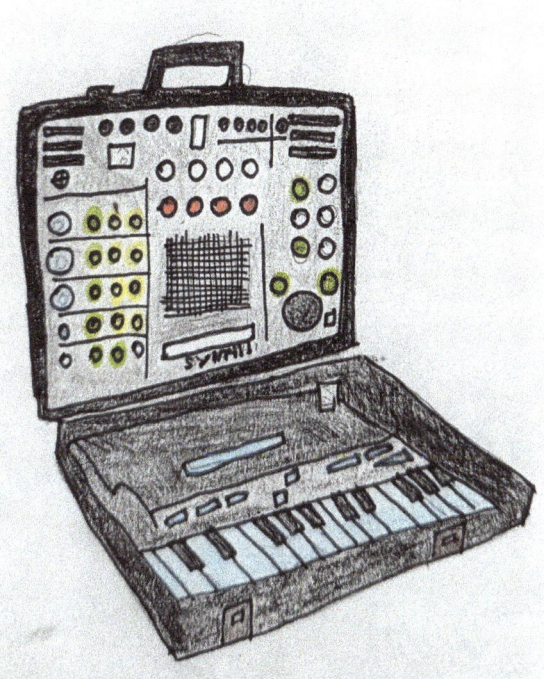

THE SUNDAY TIMES BESTSELLER

UTOPIA FOR REALISTS

AND HOW WE CAN GET THERE

RUTGER BREGMAN

BLOOMSBURY

Utopia for Beginners[1]

Out of the blue, I received an email from Luke. He had tracked down my work email address and his name popped up in my inbox. His email address was based on the name of the early Indonesian feminist, Kartini (1879-1904). I always found this a curious choice and somehow quite divergent from the person I knew: a white guy who somehow resembles Jim Carey, a couple of years older than myself and who speaks with a strong southern-US accent. Kartini's works had struck a chord with him throughout his time of living in Java.

    I had all but given up on Luke. He had become a bit of a lesson for me. After being messed around by him a few times too many some 20 years ago, I

---

[1] Written for the Reading Sideways Press blog

had drawn a line with being friends with anyone who appeared to be an alcoholic. It was the false promises and the failed meet-ups that made me ditch him as a friend.

So, these approximately 20 years had passed and then Luke contact me and told me he would pay me back the money he owed me. He explained his regret. I said no worries; but please, no sob stories. I didn't care much the cash, but I said, yes, if you want to you pay me back, yuo can. Incrementally and over a period of months, he paid me back – using Western Union.

I found it odd he would use such a money sending service, but he then informed me that he has no actual bank account. He takes regular short-term jobs, moving from state to state. He sent me a portrait of himself at a bus station about to make his latest move. He was carrying to canvas bags. He titled the photo, 'with all my belongings. The next journey.'

He has recently turned 50 and has given up alcohol. 'The funny thing is, my father also stopped drinking just before 50. He too was an alcoholic.' He tells me has no friends. He says the people he works with, are largely strung up on opioids or some other drugs. But he is clean. Luke calls me up now and then and he shares his love for the family life I have. It makes me realise again my middle-classness and privilege. I have a feeling he is getting his life back on track.

From some of the emails Luke was sending me I started to get the impression that he was getting a fair bit of exposure to the so-called alt-right. Yet, he would also express his enthusiasm and enjoyment for my own writings, which are probably written from a rather hackneyed lefty orientation. He enjoyed my articles, which he has managed to track down over the years.

I told him not to send me any of the news-material or analysis he was reading. I told him not to bother with the news: read novels instead. And so he is reading *Anna Karenina*. He sent me a WA message today, recommending me to read Voltaire's *Candide*. I think warmth and empathy shared between two old friends can help to mediate each other's extremities. I don't want to be a part of polarisation.

**

I am reading *Utopia for Realists*, yes, I am.

The title creates some kind of intuitive conflict: 'utopia' is a dream land, a non-existent place that dreamers long-for. A place in which everything works perfectly and everyone is comfortable. While self-styled 'realists' are those who espouse a somewhat pessimistic disposition; who doubt the goodness of humans. That humans always do what is in their own, immediate self-interest and who can't make long-term decisions. It's as if being a realist is synonymous with being cynical, or sceptical at best. I was enticed too by this author's Dutchness: I wanted to read something 'local', even if he is writing for a global, general audience. And for this I wouldn't be let down, for he draws on numerous examples from the Netherlands (which he calls 'Holland' in spoken interviews).

One kind of planned-Utopia is the slowly-in-progress Indonesian capital of Nusantara in East Kalimantan. A planned city that serves bureaucrats and politicians only. Bureaucrats attempt build it and then it turns out far different from the blueprints.[2]

In interviews, Bregman carries himself as a fearless debater. He is irreverent and has no truck with standard demarcations of 'left' and 'right',

---

[2] Indeed, this urban monstrosity being constructed is exactly the Utopia that Bregman writes against: "We need a new lodestar, a new map of the world that once again includes a distance, uncharted continent – "Utopia". By this I don't mean the rigid blueprints that utopian fanatics try to shove down our throats with the theocracies or their five-year plans – they only subordinate real people to fervent dreams" (p.20).

for he is contemptuous of both. The left endlessly wants more government and programs to lift the poor out of their mire, while the right are misguided for their unbridled faith in letting 'the market' just work things out. One disempowers the poor through costly and paternalistic programs; the latter lets capital reign in unequal circumstances which further disempowers those who are already marginalised. To circumvent left/right dichotomies, Bregman states how he intermingles common left/right rhetoric: being nationalist and being pro-gay marriage for example. 'I'm proud of country for we were the first to legalise gay marriage', he says.

Bregman is writing from a utopia he refers to as The Land of Plenty where society is advanced and wealthy. It is where things are undoubtedly much better in the past when '99% of humanity was poor, hungry, dirty, afraid, stupid, sick and ugly' (p.1). Unlike other critical texts on contemporary social-political conditions, Bregman is not starting out from a perspective that things are going to hell in a handbasket. Bregman spends the first few pages describing how good we have it compared to the olden days: long-lives, recreation, low-murder rates, social nets (if you have the right passport);

lower rates of malnutrition; hundreds of millions of people "being lifted out of extreme poverty" (p.6).

One of Bregman's truths he seeks to upset is in regards to the kinds of work that are valued. He seeks to disturb the belief that because someone is well-paid, the job the person performs is valuable. Or at least, essential to a society's general quality of life. Bregman holds particular contempt for bankers; particularly the kind that take risks with *other people's money* and whom are rewarded with large bonuses. He bemoans the kinds of work which don't create anything of value, yet merely shift money throughout the economy. On the other hand, he frequently builds his arguments around the value created by folks in poorly paid professions: teachers, nurses and garbage collectors.

Probably Bregman is at his best in interviews. It is in such spaces that he can confront and contest his opponent's (or host's) preconceived ideas. *Utopia for Realists* outlines his thinking fair and reasonably but it lacks some of the vivacity and bite of his oral performance.

**

No doubt Luke didn't always do the best by himself. But I also think that his country also didn't do the best for him. Bregman frequently chimes in with damning statistics and stories which describes the inequality and gap between rich and poor in the US.

I had always felt that Luke had well and truly fallen through the cracks in the metaphorical floor. When I told a friend about Luke's situation, he upped my metaphor and said, 'there was no floor to begin with'.

Luke may well be one of the kinds of persons who would benefit greatly from a Bregmanesque universal basic income. This would prevent him from having to shift around the States in search of the next seasonal job that can string him along for the next few months or so. Bregman refers to the unqualified basic income as start-up, basic venture capital which can enable those with a lack of cash to make better, longer-term decisions and invest in their own future. I'm grateful for Luke's friendship, for he was once lost to me – and probably also himself.

'A book that should be available on the NHS'
EMERALD STREET

HOW TO
BREAK UP
WITH YOUR
PHONE

THE 30-DAY PLAN TO
TAKE BACK YOUR LIFE
CATHERINE PRICE

DR EMILY GROSSMAN
BRAIN-FIZZING FACTS

AWESOME SCIENCE QUESTIONS ANSWERED

BLOOMSBURY

ILLUSTRATED BY ALICE BOWSHER

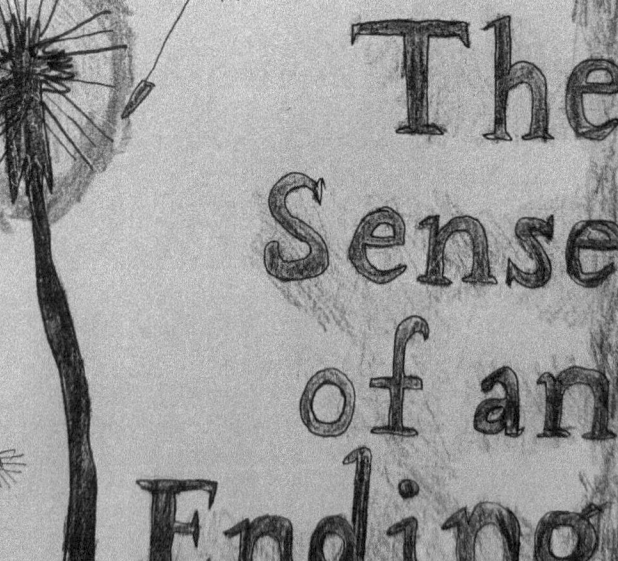

After-word

Towards the end of preparing this text, I picked up a book by James C. Scott and in the introduction he writes, "I'm the only one to blame for this book." I feel a little bit the same way about this little book. It is my deliberate act of writing folly.

While I aim to be the only one to be blamed for this book, I have gleaned my inspiration from growing up in a house with walls lined with books (and paintings): the collection(s) of Michele and Trevor. My father bought books with the imagination of creating a library and thus there are thousands of books on the shelves in their home. Some are lent out to family members. Trev rearranges their position on the shelves when he finds new categories in which to put them; when they find new friends to be associated with. My mother would recount the novels she read in five minute summaries. I wonder what stories she would write, if *the accident wills* her to do so.

I'm frequently surprised and inspired by my partner Nuraini's austere reading. She is particularly selective in what she reads and I find she turns her readings into multiple texts. It is as if a few articles or chapters or a book are able to propel much thinking and even more words. Nuraini is particularly economical with her reading, while I feel a little inclined towards proliferating the kinds of books I read. The process of drawing covers taught me, a little, to decentre my tastes and to read authors whose works I had long seen on bookshop shelves but never bought. Nonetheless, I still find my prejudices rudely interfere with which books I pick up.

**

I first started using the term for a 'reading sideways' blog in 2013 when we moved to Leiden soon after our daughter was born. It was a small, unstructured blog, which after a while turned into readingsideways.net which focused on sports culture. I used readingsideways.net to mainly write about football fandom in Indonesia. The articles have now been incorporated into readingsidewayspress.com

The term 'reading sideways' was something that I had adapted from reading Henk Maier's book, *We are playing relatives* (KITLV, 2004). Henk is a professor of comparative literature in California but was previously' the professor of Indonesian literature at Leiden University. Somehow I felt that reading sideways evoked Maier's approach to literary and writing practices. He perpetually looked beyond his texts at hand. Maybe there is little 'original' – to borrow James C. Scott's own self-criticism - in this approach specifically, but it struck me at the time. Maier brought other matters into the mix of his analysis and seemed to pay much attention to his own style. Although hardly a bestseller, it is anything but a staid and dry academic treatise. Much of the Indonesian (literary) studies writing only drew on other work by Indonesian studies scholars. Henk through many other writers into the mix. When reading his works, it didn't feel like 'writing in Malay from the Archipelago' was so separated from things happening elsewhere.

As well as this 'sideways' glance to other *elsewheres*, I also felt he engaged with the context in which authors wrote and publishers published in a lively manner. *We are playing relatives* is not only a tome on olden and present days writing, but also is a kind of confession of Henk's own reading and writing practices and he reveals the function reading plays for him.

I didn't mean to write this book. It is not the book I intended to write. But here it is.

I have now finished this book.

Leiden, 16th September 2023

Seeing Like a State

How Certain Schemes to Improve the
Human Condition Have Failed

James C Scott

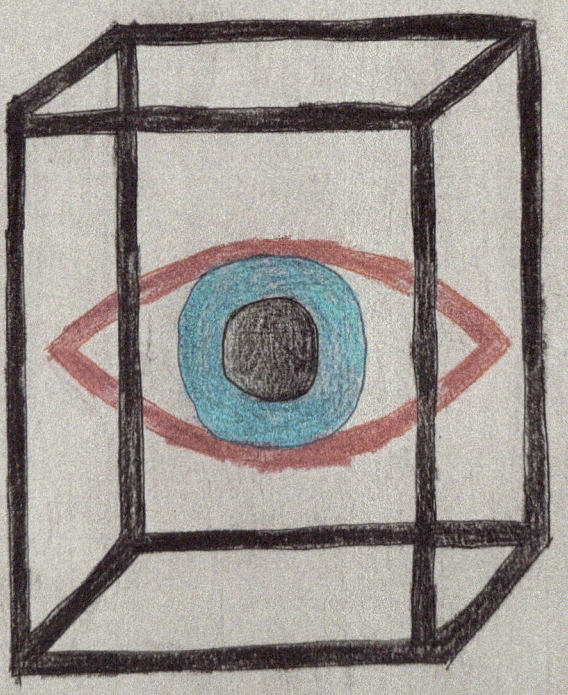

Book List

Benjamin, Walter (2015), *Illuminations*, London: The Bodley Head.

Calvino, Italo (1992) *If on a Winter's Night a Traveller, trans. William Weaver*, London: Vintage Classics

Coote, James (1968), *Olympic Report 1968*, London: Robert Hale.

Edwards, Harry (2017), *The Revolt of the Black Athlete: 50th Anniversary Edition, with a new introduction and afterword*, Urbana: University of Chicago Press.

Eenvoudig Communiceren (ed.) (2010), *Brieven aan de prinses*, Amsterdam: Eenvoudig Communiceren.

Ellenberg, Jordan (2015), *How Not to be Wrong*, London: Penguin.

Gaiman, Neil (2001). *American Gods: The Author's Preferred Text*. London: Headline.

Gaiman, Neil (2005). *Anansi Boys*. London: Headline.

Gaiman, Neil (2000). *Neverwhere*. London: Headline.

Ghosh, Amitav (2021), *The Nutmeg's Curse: Parables for a Planet in Crisis*, Chicago: University of Chicago Press.

Hobsbawm, E.J. (1969), *Bandits*, London: Weidenfeld & Nicolson.

Kinney, Jeff (2007), *Diary of a Wimpy Kid: a novel in cartoons*, New York: Amulet Books.

Le Guin, Ursula K. (1987), *Buffalo Gals and Other Animal Presences*, Santa Barbara: Capra Press

Lockhart, Greg (2023), *Weaving of Worlds: a Day on Île d'Yeu*, Leiden: Reading Sideways Press.

Lucashenko, Melissa (2013), *Mullumbimby,* St Lucia: University of Queensland Press

Malna, Afrizal (1984). *ABAD YANG BERLARI*, Jakarta: Lembaga Penerbit Altermed Yayasan Lingkaran Merahputih.

Malna, Afrizal (2002), *Dalam Rahim Ibuku Tak ada Anjing*, Yogyakarta: Bentang.

Malna Afrizal (2004). *Lubang dari Separuh Langit*. Yogyakarta: AKY Press.

Malna, Afrizal (2021), *Morning Slanting to the Right*, Richmond: Reading Sideways Press.

Malna, Afrizal (2020), *Prometheus Pinball*, Richmond: Reading Sideways Press.

Malna, Afrizal (1990), *Yang Berdiam Dalam Mikropon*, Jakarta: Medan Sastra Indonesia.

Price, Catherine (2018), *How to Break Up With Your Phone: The 30-Day Plan to Take Back Your Life*, Berkeley: Ten Speed Press.

Scott, James C. (2020), *Seeing Like a State: How Certain Schemes to Improve the Human Condition Have Failed*, New Haven: Yale University Press.

Schütte, Uwe (2020), *Kraftwerk: Future Music from Germany,* London: Penguin.

Simone, AbdouMaliq (2009), *City Life from Jakarta to Dakar: Movements at the Crossroads*, London: Routledge

Simone, AbdouMaliq (2014), *Jakarta: Drawing the City Near*, Minneapolis: University of Minnesota Press.

Simatupang, Iwan (1975), *Kooong*, Jakarta: Pustaka Jaya.

Simatupang, Iwan (1977), *Merahnya Merah: Sebuh Novel*, Jakarta: Gunung Agung.

Solemanto (2009), *K.H.A. Fadloli El Muhir: Jejak Langkah Sang Kiai, Mengawal Republik dari Tanah Betawi*, Jakarta: Pondok Pesantren Ziyadatul Mubtadi'ien.

Terstappen, Claudia (2014). *House of Collections: Photographs of 11 Barina Road, Glen Iris*. 20 Copies only: Artist's book.

Verdery, Katherine (2018). *My Life as a Spy: Investigations in a Secret Police File*. Durham: Duke University Press.

www.ingramcontent.com/pod-product-compliance
Lightning Source LLC
Chambersburg PA
CBHW040741020526
44107CB00084B/2833